God
Between
the Covers

Other Books by Marcia Ford

Memoir of a Misfit:
Finding My Place in the Family of God

Meditations for Misfits:
Finding Your Place in the Family of God

101 Most Powerful Promises in the Bible

Restless Pilgrim:
The Spiritual Journey of Bob Dylan
(with Scott Marshall)

Checklist for Life for Teens

Checklist for Life for Graduates

Checklist for Life for Teachers

Checklist for Life for Leaders
(with Angie Kiesling)

God
Between
the Covers

Finding Faith
Through Reading

Marcia Ford

A Crossroad Book
The Crossroad Publishing Company
New York

The Crossroad Publishing Company
16 Penn Plaza – 481 Eighth Avenue, Suite 1550
New York, NY 10001

Printed in the United States of America

The text of this book is set in 11/16 Bembo.
The display faces are Calligraphic 421 and Caxton.

Library of Congress Cataloging-in-Publication Data
Ford, Marcia.
    God between the covers : finding faith through reading /
Marcia Ford.
      p. cm.
    Includes bibliographical references (p.) and index.
    ISBN 0-8245-2290-7 (alk. paper)
    1. Books and reading – Religious aspects – Christianity.
2. Christian literature – History and criticism.   I. Title.
BR117.F67 2005
261.5′8 – dc22
                                    2005022082

1 2 3 4 5 6 7 8 9 10   10 09 08 07 06 05

To Roberta Radcliffe Budmen,
a teacher who made me feel cherished

Contents

God
Between
the Covers

Introduction

A Little More
Than a Preference

It's hardly surprising that some of the best memories of my adult life center on an apartment I rented in an older Victorian house in Ocean Grove, New Jersey. A tiny balcony in front overlooked a murky lake whose muddy water couldn't hide the rusting shopping carts lurking near the surface. But if I lifted my eyes the slightest bit, I had a perfect view of one of Asbury Park's many wonderland attractions: White's Galleries, home to so many used books that the proprietor couldn't keep up with his inventory. Legend has it that one of my professors found a first-edition Mark Twain carelessly tossed onto one of the many stacks that lined the shrinking aisles between the book tables in the center and the bookshelves along the wall.

These days, I have little need to ever enter a bookstore. As a book reviewer, a judge for several book awards, and a writer for a publishing trade magazine, I need do no more than answer the door to acquire more books than I could read in their entirety in a lifetime. FedEx and UPS long ago gave up ringing my doorbell; under our standing agreement, they just drop and run. They know I'll check my porch like clockwork, three times every weekday. And more often than not, a fresh supply of books will be there waiting for me.

Yet I cannot stay away from bookstores any more than I can give up my three mugs of coffee each morning. That's what addiction is, after all: a need, not simply a preference. That's why, when I make the six-hour drive to my beloved prayer center in southern Georgia, I take a driving break and leave the interstate not at an exit where I could get a decent meal but where there's an outlet center boasting two bookstores. And that's another aspect of addiction: you can't be choosy when you need a fix. I prefer Folgers and a quaint little bookshop, but I'll gladly settle for a drive-thru brew and a book warehouse.

This addiction to books, I think, pretty much started the day I realized I could read on my own, and it very nearly was broken by a public school system determined to make the act of reading as boring as possible. If not for Nancy Drew and *Teen* magazine, I might have lost my taste for reading at a much too tender age. But like my addiction to caffeine, which returned as soon as I resumed drinking coffee after both my pregnancies, my need to read came back despite the hiatus. It returned during college, when I often had to read entire books and not just excerpts in textbooks. That was a skill I had nearly lost.

◆ ◆ ◆

Back in the spring of 1972, I was in my senior year of college, out of work, and living on food stamps. More often than not, I had to borrow money for gas to get to campus. For four weeks in a row, my ever-suffering landlady had patiently listened to each excuse I offered for why I could not pay the rent. About the only thing that saved me from eviction was her long memory and her maternal love. She had once been a cash-strapped college student, and now her son was one as well. My cash, of course, would have made him less strapped, but she graciously avoided pointing that out.

I don't recall if she was home one day when I walked through the door toting a shopping bag from a nearby store. If so, she never mentioned it. Maybe she assumed the bag was filled with required reading for one of my courses, or maybe she was too busy filling out loan forms so she could send her son some lunch money. I like to think she secretly shared my addiction and averted her eyes out of respect.

Two details I do remember from that day are the titles of the books I bought — one being *Only One Year* by Svetlana Alliluyeva, daughter of Joseph Stalin — and the store where I bought them. In fact, I suspect that for many of the books on my sagging bookcases, I can clearly recall the exact circumstances that compelled me to buy them, right down to the way they were positioned on the bookstore shelf or haphazardly piled on the remainder table.

On this day, I had ended up in Belmar, New Jersey, halfheartedly looking for a job, having convinced myself I had saturated all the employment possibilities in Asbury Park where I lived. Well, if I was going to waste gas looking for a job, I was certainly going to make it worthwhile. So in between filling out job applications — the plural there is doubtful — I wandered in and out of every store that sold books. I discovered Svetlana in a clothing store, of all places, along with Aleksandr Solzhenitsyn's *One Day in the Life of Ivan Denisovich*. I imagine the owner to have been a Russian émigré who found great delight in two authors from her homeland whose anti-Communist writings attracted an international audience — and the scorn of the Soviet government. None of that mattered much to me. I was on a Russian roll at the time, and there were two books I'd long wanted to read. I bought both.

Today it astounds me that I never thought twice about that purchase. What I spent on those books that day probably represented my grocery money for the week. I don't think I need to go into detail about my book-buying habits once I graduated from college and got a real job with a steady paycheck.

◆ ◆ ◆

If college reignited my addiction, the church added fuel to that fire. Both my reading and my lifestyle during college made me realize the extent to which I had lost my moorings. Exposure to so many new and exciting and challenging ideas in print had made me fairly susceptible to adopting a worldview that in the end was somewhere between contradictory and illogical. I didn't just want it both ways; I wanted it *all* ways. Today, I can't even begin to define that worldview.

Something was radically wrong, and I knew it had to do with truth and relativity, authority and authenticity. Was everything relative, as some said? Where was the line between questioning authority, which we in the counterculture were encouraged to do, and defying authority? Or was there no line? Who has authority, anyway? And if something looked and smelled and tasted authentic, did that mean it was true?

I needed my moorings, and I had a clue where I had left them. I returned to church and became tethered to those moorings once again. I read the Bible for the first time as an adult and found it to be both profound and perplexing, which meant it was time for more reading. I read books about the Bible and books about books about the Bible. I read books about people in the Bible and books about people who wrote about people in the Bible. I bought books by the armful. As a matter of self-preservation, I developed my own method of speed-reading.

I had found truth. I had found an authority I could trust. I had found authenticity.

Or had I? After a quarter century of immersion in the things of the Spirit, variations of those old questions began to nag at me: Was everything relative after all? How big was the gap between questioning authority, which we in the church were discouraged from doing, and blindly obeying authority? Who really has authority? And if something looked and smelled and tasted authentic, did that mean it was true?

◆ ◆ ◆

Soon enough, someone identified my theological malady as "postmodernism." On the one hand, I was flattered: I belonged! For a self-proclaimed misfit, this was good news indeed. On the other hand, I was bewildered. Sure, I had a passable understanding of what postmoderns believe, but did I truly qualify as one? It was clearly time to investigate this latter-day phenomenon on a deeper level. Which meant I had yet another reason to buy more books. As those who have helped me move my belongings will confirm, I will take on any research project that comes with a license to buy more books, especially if they are tax-deductible.

My bookshelves were already complaining under the weight of so many postmodern / emerging church volumes, but the standards of thorough research — my

standards, anyway — dictated the amassing of a comprehensive library dedicated to the topic at hand. None of
this helped me get a better handle on how I fit in as a
postmodernist, of course, but it gave me the research
fix I needed. And it provided me with untold hours of
great and not-so-great reading as I made my way through
the piles of books on my floor, which lent a certain intellectual ambience to my home even as my feng shui
sensibilities blanched in horror. Maybe *that's* my personal
expression of postmodernism: a sort of intellectual feng
shui — cerebral and emotive.

Anyone who doesn't know me may be picturing a
home with a special room filled with leather-bound
books — a dark, very British library, perhaps, with built-
in bookcases lining the richly paneled walls and two
sinfully comfortable overstuffed chairs flanking a roar-
ing fireplace. Those who do know me picture the actual
mess my motley assortment of books has made of our
small ranch house in Florida. The volumes in the living room alone range from children's Golden Books and
garishly colored picture books, to broken-spined mass-
market paperback novels and Ann Rule's true crimes, to
a preponderance of trade paperbacks and hardbacks, and,
finally, to one or two impressive-looking leather-bound
titles. Just inside the front door, there's a Bible...in
manuscript form — fifteen hundred loose pages shipped
to me in an oversized carton by a publisher who must

have thought I needed it. I have no idea what to do with it, so there it sits.

Hidden in this mass of several thousand books are an untold number of works that have truly helped me in my personal and spiritual formation. I will never know exactly how many have influenced my life in a significant way. Who's to say how much *Little Women* influenced me, though today I only remember it as an enjoyable read? Maybe Jane Austen's books have affected me on some deep spiritual level more than I know, though I've never enjoyed them much at all.

But there are some whose impact is so evident that I can say with confidence that these are the books that shaped my life — powerful, influential, life-changing books with staying power. Those are the books you'll find in the pages to come — places where I discovered the evidence of God between the covers of a book.

One

A SEPARATE PEACE

Fiction and the Spiritual Search

The combined forces of the public school system and an unthinking relative who derisively called me a bookworm pretty much killed my early interest in reading. I figured out how to get good grades without doing much work, which also meant without doing a whole lot of reading. That changed in college. I had to read, and I had to read a lot. Soon enough, my latent passion for books had returned. My latent passion for God would take longer. But I began to notice his fingerprints all over the books I was reading. I wanted him to go away and leave me alone. But no. God would turn up again and again in literature, which as an English major I couldn't exactly escape. If I had been honest with myself, which at the time I struggled mightily not to be, I would have admitted my inability to live without God and conceded the victory to him much sooner than I did.

In those days I was what I call a prepostmodern: someone whose way of thinking would eventually be defined
as postmodern but who felt forced to conform to a thoroughly modern world. On the surface, I bought into the
modern reliance on technology and science and certainty,
but deep down, I questioned most of what I appeared
so certain about. Toward the end of my college years,
I would finally confront the tension between *theological*
certainty and doubt that had plagued me since junior
high school.

This is the point at which I should offer a dictionary-
like definition of theological postmodernism. I'm going
to forgo that, since words are subject to nearly endless
interpretation, which actually limits communication. I'm
generally up for a spirited discussion on the nuances of
a particular word but not when said discussion gets in
the way of more important things, like the future of the
church, for instance. We need to find one term to use for
the long haul, and "postmodern" fits that bill just fine.
We're in the embryonic phase of what may prove to be
a revolutionary change, and it's too soon to start fiddling
with semantics.

What I *can* do, here and in the chapters to come, is offer
an unofficial glimpse into the way I see Christian postmodernism lived out in everyday life: by modeling an
authentic faith, becoming — and remaining — culturally
relevant, being open to changing the way we do church,
serving others in body, mind, and spirit, expressing our

spirituality in creative ways, and allowing ourselves and others to openly question those things we were once so certain about.

But back to 1968 and my first year at Monmouth College. These are some of the writings through which God began to reveal himself to me over the next four years. They provided a stable foundation for the framework of my faith to come.

John Knowles 📖

A Separate Peace

So few people ever talk about this book that I was beginning to wonder if Monmouth College was the only school in the 1970s that continued to require its reading. In the context of the Vietnam conflict, John Knowles's coming-of-age story set during World War II provided a framework and a place for me to come to terms with the conflicting philosophies and opinions and emotions I was grappling with at the time. It was an unlikely pairing, the students at the center of *A Separate Peace* and me. Gene and Finny were two privileged teenage guys in a prep school during a war that was almost universally supported at home, and I was a less-than-privileged young woman on a college scholarship during a highly unpopular war. I suspect many students today would have a difficult time grasping the relevance of this story to their lives, yet its relevance was probably even less apparent on the surface back in the Vietnam era.

What made a profound impression on me was the conflict between living by the rules, embodied in the point-of-view character of Gene, and living by the gut, a skill that Gene's roommate, Finny, had clearly mastered. Finny exposed the mass of contradictions that character-ized many of us. Finny put feet to the rebel within, but he did so in such a disarming manner that his rebellion against the school's rigidity seldom cost him anything. That's what I wanted, rebellion minus the price tag, re-bellion that would, in fact, make me more likable and popular.

Among Finny's contradictions was his attitude toward the war, a war that at times he didn't "believe in." What he didn't believe in were the reports of the American bomb-ing raids. We had no problem believing similar reports during Vietnam; what we didn't believe were the denials of horrific incidents like the My Lai massacre. Yet, like Finny — who tried to enlist in a war he didn't believe to be real — I had to be honest and admit that I didn't see the war as a black-and-white issue. There was much too much gray obscuring the truth at the time.

There is a striking element of postmodernism to Finny's thought processes and behavior. He had created his own reality — a "separate peace," as it were — by liv-ing in the moment. That specific concept wasn't clear to me at the time; all I knew was, this guy enjoyed life in a way that I envied. Down deep, I was much too much like Gene, always worrying about the next exam, though unlike Gene I never admitted that to anyone else. Unlike the proverbial kid in timeout who is sitting on the outside but standing up on the inside, I was the kid standing up on the outside but obediently sitting down on the inside.

God made a cameo appearance in *A Separate Peace* when Finny voiced the opinion that people should pray in case it turns out that there really is a God. I disagreed. I figured there probably was a God, but my prayers, should I choose to utter them, would fall on his deaf ears.

A Separate Peace, by John Knowles (New York: Macmillan, 1967).

Gerard Manley Hopkins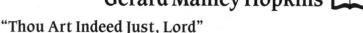
"Thou Art Indeed Just, Lord"

I recently read an excellent book, *Why Men Hate Going to Church*, in which author Dave Murrow suggests that churches hold more activities and services outdoors because men tend to find God more readily in nature than inside a building. Which makes me curious about my own testosterone level; is there an easy way of checking that out, using a kind of hormonal dipstick? Just wondering, because I've always found God more accessible outdoors. In fact, the moment when I finally became convinced of God's existence and active involvement in my life occurred on a mountainside in Vermont, not in a church building.

Gerard Manley Hopkins so believed that all of nature provided irrefutable evidence of God that many of his poems echo those Psalms that testify to the natural world's proclamation of God: "The world is charged with the grandeur of God," he writes in "God's Grandeur," about as close as you can get to "The heavens declare the handiwork of God" in Psalm 19 without crossing the plagiarism line. In college, it was that "God in nature" aspect of Hopkins's poetry that caught my eye, since I did not know God the way he did — Hopkins being a Jesuit and me being a...whatever I was. (In *All Saints*, Robert Ellsberg describes Hopkins's decision to join the Society of Jesus as a "move tantamount, in polite society, to joining a bizarre and foreign cult.") I was best described as a skeptic, I guess. I knew something was out there that was bigger than us, but to call that something God made that something more personal than I wanted to think about.

In the poem "Inversnaid," Hopkins defends the natural world from the encroachment of humanity:

> *What would the world be, once bereft*
> *Of wet and of wildness? Let them be left,*
> *O let them be left, wildness and wet;*
> *Long live the weeds and the wilderness yet.*

I can now find God in a well-tended garden, but like Hopkins I prefer nature's wildness. The Hopkins lines I turn to most frequently these days, however, contain no references to nature:

> *Thou art indeed just, Lord, if I contend*
> *With thee; but, sir, so what I plead is just.*
> *Why do sinners' ways prosper? And why must*
> *Disappointment all I endeavour end?*
> *Wert thou my enemy, O thou my friend,*
> *How wouldst thou worse, I wonder, than thou dost*
> *Defeat, thwart me?*

In other words, "Why, O God, why?" My sentiments exactly.

Modern American & Modern British Poetry, ed. Louis Untermeyer (New York: Harcourt, Brace, 1955).

Fyodor Dostoyevsky 📖

Crime and Punishment

Never mind the fact that the premise of *Crime and Punishment* offered strong support for one of Stalin's worst ideas. Fyodor Dostoyevsky's masterpiece of Russian literature — no, world literature — resounds with a message of hope that regenerated Christians have long been preaching, whether through their words or through their lives. Hope may not be the word that comes to mind when this novel is mentioned, but stay with me for a while.

Stalin's idea, which was not exactly original with him, was that an extended stay in a prison work camp in the godforsaken wasteland known as Siberia would turn a very bad man into a very obedient subject of the Russian state. Or, to Stalin's way of thinking, a very good man. Stalin's opinions aside, the protagonist of *Crime and Punishment,* Raskolnikov — is that a great name or what? — finds the redemption that eludes him throughout much of the book when he at last begins to live out his sentence in a Siberian prison camp.

Unlike so many other imprisoned heroes of fiction, Raskolnikov actually committed the crime he was convicted of. Convinced that some people are naturally superior to others, and that he was among the superior breed, Raskolnikov set out to prove that theory by plotting and committing the murder of an old woman, a scurrilous pawnbroker who was so corrupt that he considered her death to be a benefit to society. And he continued to try to prove his superiority by playing mind games with the police — until he met his match in a detective named Porfiry, thus setting up a relationship that would live on in a modified form in every single episode of *Columbo.*

Back to Raskolnikov, who eventually realized he was not all that great. His guilt over the murder led to intense suffering, which gave Dostoyevsky an opportunity to write one of the most memorable descriptions ever of a person wracked with the feverish, debilitating symptoms of a guilt-induced illness. Following his recovery, Raskolnikov tried to live with the guilt, but he began lusting after some form of punishment that would free him from the prison he had built for himself. He eventually confessed. Siberia became a symbol of freedom for him.

So where does the message of hope come in? I find it in his release from the guilt that had consumed him, a release so transforming that not even eight years in a prison camp could contain his joy. I think of Raskolnikov whenever I meet people whose attempts to justify their actions only drive them deeper and deeper into their own despair. I'm well aware that guilt isn't a popular subject, just as sin isn't a word people like to use in polite conversation. Call it what you may, but people weighed down by guilt don't suddenly get over it when you try to tell them that sin doesn't exist. Me, I'd hand them a copy of *Crime and Punishment* instead.

Crime and Punishment, by Fyodor Dostoyevsky (New York: Oxford University Press, 1953).

Francis Thompson 📖
"The Hound of Heaven"

Eight years after I walked away from church, convinced that organized religion was only interfering with my relationship with God, I sat in a pot-induced haze in a college classroom pondering the weightier issues of life. Or so I'd like to believe. More likely, my attention was fixated on the many trappings of wealth that surrounded me; my classroom had once been the formal dining room in Woodrow Wilson's summer home during his presidency. If you've seen the movie *Annie,* you've seen Wilson Hall, the building that housed the English department at Monmouth College (now a university) in New Jersey. It served as the set for Daddy Warbucks's palatial home in that movie.

It was during one of those hazy class times that one of the first real miracles of my adult life occurred. You may balk at that word "miracle," and I don't blame you. All I can do is describe what happened and declare it a miracle, which by my definition is an incident that can only be explained in supernatural terms; the laws of nature are suspended, and the supernatural intervenes. The laws of nature would agree that I was stoned that day. But we were reading Francis Thompson in English Lit class, and the supernatural — God — intervened, and I understood Thompson's words with clarity.

We — or rather, they — began discussing "The Hound of Heaven," Thompson's poem about God's relentless pursuit of him despite his every effort to run from God. I'm sure we were supposed to read the poem before class, and I'm equally sure I did not. As I sat in class, not only did my head clear up, but the barriers I had built against anything smacking of religion came crashing down.

> *I fled Him, down the nights and down the days;*
> *I fled Him, down the arches of the years;*
> *I fled Him, down the labyrinthine ways*
> *Of my own mind; and in the mist of tears*
> *I hid from Him, and under running laughter.*

Thompson's words became mine; I owned them, and I owned up to them. Yes, I had been fleeing, hiding, running.

> *(For though I knew His love Who followed,*
> *Yet I was sore adread*
> *Lest, having Him, I must have naught beside.)*

Indeed. Having God meant relinquishing all else. I knew that. So I fled, I hid, I ran.

> *How little worthy of any love thou art!*
> *Whom wilt thou find to love ignoble thee,*
> *Save Me, save only Me?*

I offered no protest to that.

> *All which I took from thee I did but take,*
> *Not for thy harms,*
> *But just that thou might'st seek it in My arms.*

By now I was spent, drained. The Hound of Heaven had indeed been dogging me, tracking me down the many labyrinthine paths I'd taken, nipping at my heels, sniffing me out of all those hiding places I thought I'd been so clever to find.

It would be another two years before I would eventually trade in my life on the lam for one of "naught beside." But during those final years of fleeing, hiding, running, I found a certain measure of satisfaction in knowing that my relentless pursuer had an identity I could understand. He was the Hound of Heaven — Thompson's Hound of Heaven, and mine as well.

Modern American & Modern British Poetry, ed. Louis Untermeyer (New York: Harcourt, Brace, 1955).

📖 The Poetry of Robert Frost

You know how some music sounds so — so *eternal?* Beethoven and Bach immediately come to mind, but so do *Days of Future Passed* by the Moody Blues and the score to *Dances with Wolves.* The print counterpart to that kind of music is poetry that carries an infinite ring in its sound, even if you only hear it in your head. That's what I love most about Robert Frost's poems. The man could put sounds together that created a symphony of words rivaling the work of any musical composer. In those sounds, I hear God.

Take "Stopping by Woods on a Snowy Evening," which I happen to appreciate for its meaning and imagery as much as its sound. The title alone is lyrical. Add lines like these: "Between the woods and frozen lake/The darkest evening of the year" or "The only other sound's the sweep/Of easy wind and downy flake" — and I find myself believing in God all over again, just like the first time. See, I can't imagine language just happening, and I sure can't see it just happening with such an array of exquisite sounds that can be combined in such exquisite ways. (And that goes for every language, including — I'm dead serious here — German. Guttural *ist gut* in the right context.)

Another favorite, "Birches," gets mixed up in my head with a James Taylor song that mentions birches and that I dare not quote, what with ASCAP creating an accounting nightmare every time a line from a song appears in print. One thing I don't get confused about is these lines from Frost, not Taylor: "I'd like to get away from earth awhile/And then come back to it and begin over." Those lines appeal to me less because of their sound and more because that's what I feel like doing most days. But the poem continues and gets decidedly lyrical:

> *I'd like to go by climbing a birch tree*
> *And climb black branches up a snow-white trunk*
> Toward *heaven, till the tree could bear no more,*
> *But dipped its top and set me down again.*

I recall a study done decades ago that determined that the most beautiful-sounding words in the English language were "cellar door," despite the mundane image those words convey. I don't remember how the researchers came to that conclusion; did they use some kind of high-tech instruments, or did they test a scientific sampling of the general public? I'm guessing the instruments were manufactured in Rome or the public sampling included a high percentage of Italian-Americans, because "cellar door" sure sounds Italian to me. No matter. All I know is, Robert Frost could take the words "cellar door" and turn them into a magnificent symphony of sound.

The Poetry of Robert Frost, ed. Edward Connery Lathem (New York: Holt, Rinehart and Winston, 1969).

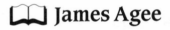 # James Agee

A Death in the Family

The greatest sorrow I would ever know was years ahead of me the first time I read James Agee's masterpiece. Yet, even in the years immediately following, when the only grief in my life was the kind my roommates gave me, I felt as if I had somehow known the kind of grief Agee wrote about. I hadn't, but he convinced me that some universal truths need not be experienced in order to know that they are true; rather, there's a kind of universal knowing of these truths residing deep inside us long before they become operative in our lives.

No novel before or since *A Death in the Family* — at least, no novel I'm aware of — has surpassed this extraordinary glimpse into the ordinariness of death. Agee reveals the internal thoughts and fears and concerns of several family members, both nuclear and extended, and how they affect the dynamics of the grieving process. And he brings faith into the picture without forcing it on the story, through some characters who believe and others who do not — or who say they do not believe or believe they do not believe.

Agee apparently couldn't resist taking a swipe at the institutional church by demonstrating how a misguided cleric can sometimes trample all over an authentic personal faith in God. I silently cheered at his frequent use of the word "displeased" to describe Father Jackson's expressions and demeanor. That's a word that perfectly fits my memories of way too many pastors. Their displeasure at the comings and goings and normal lives of the laity was all too evident on their faces.

Though faith is evident in the story, it's the ordinariness of death that remains in the forefront, never better depicted than in a scene in which Andrew, a brother-in-law of the deceased, walks home with lines from "O Little Town of Bethlehem" inexplicably intruding on his thoughts. The results of death, Agee shows, are often weird and quirky and border on bizarre.

Some editions of the book include portions that Agee was working on at the time of his death but had not inserted into the text. The edition I have inserts those portions where the editors believe Agee would have placed them and sets them apart with italics. Maybe it's just me, but I don't see how they bring anything significant to the story, and at times they almost feel as if they're a part of another book entirely. I quickly realized my enjoyment and appreciation of the book would be better served if I just ignored them.

Another Agee classic is *Let Us Now Praise Famous Men,* a nonfiction account of the lives of several sharecropper families, illustrated through the photography of Walker Evans. (Don't get me started on the power of photography, or this will end up as *God through the Lenses.*) The strange thing about this particular book is that the title evokes such an upwelling of recalled emotion within me, yet when I look at the book today, it does nothing for me. I can't explain it. I know it's a marvelous book. I know it meant a great deal to me earlier in my life. Today, nothing. But I'm thinking it's still worth recommending.

A Death in the Family, by James Agee (New York: Random House/Vintage, 1985).

📖 Franz Kafka

The Trial

So there are a few odd titles in my memory bank, but surely this must be the oddest when it comes to finding

God between the covers of a book. Where on earth is God in this frightening look at the absurdity and inhumanity of a modern world run by bureaucrats?

The Trial, which traces the descent of an ordinary bank clerk following his arrest on unnamed charges, is the quintessential — dare I say it? — Kafkaesque novel, a depiction of the nightmarish quality of everyday life. Josef K. is thwarted at every turn in his efforts to find out what he has done wrong — or more accurately, what someone thinks he has done wrong. The nightmare of bureaucratic red tape wreaks havoc on his mind. And he begins to feel guilty. It only gets worse from there.

The absence of God makes the need for God all the more evident. That was what I sensed in my first reading of *The Trial*. It was just too creepy, too disturbing, too potentially prophetic for me to accept. No way could we let our lives — here in the land of the free and the home of the brave! — ever become that bleak. I'm telling you, I nearly got down on my knees and prayed a variation on what I call the Wizard of Oz prayer: "I do believe in God! I do believe in God! I do I do I do I do believe in God!" Not witches — God! And I wasn't even sure God was a *benevolent* God at the time.

The Trial, by Franz Kafka (New York: Schocken Books, 1968).

📖 Nathaniel Hawthorne

The Scarlet Letter

A little knowledge is indeed a dangerous thing. "It's a red-letter day," I heard my fifth-grade teacher say to the sixth-grade teacher, and for months afterward, I quaked at the thought of what her ominous words really meant. What terror had befallen our little school? A red letter, as everyone knows, is a scarlet letter, and I knew enough to know that the words "scarlet letter" referred to something dreadful and sinful. Thinking back on it today, I realize how odd it is that I was more familiar with something called *The Scarlet Letter* than I was with the common phrase "red-letter day."

Familiarity is indeed a strange thing. I have no doubt that it breeds contempt, but I've also seen it breed indifference. Seriously, after becoming all too familiar with Hester Prynne and the Reverend Arthur Dimmesdale and Roger Chillingworth — the three main characters in *The Scarlet Letter* — during their school years, how many people want to go back and reread that all-too-familiar story? As usual, I'm the odd one out. Because I wanted to, and I did. While others carried the memory of Hester Prynne (another great name!) as a wanton woman, I saw her as a flawed but strong and courageous woman.

Most of all, *The Scarlet Letter* is a story of redemption — for Hester, Arthur, and their daughter, Pearl — and a story of hope. After suffering years of public humiliation and shame, Hester turned her ignominy into a ministry to the equally downtrodden. If the truth were known, I'm convinced we would discover a host of women whose sordid past has crippled them and prevented them from feeling in any way useful to God. And what do you want to bet these same women read *The Scarlet Letter* in school? Okay, so maybe they didn't all read it, but most of them probably at least read a synopsis. But all they came away with was a snicker and a vague memory that the book was about sex. Which is precisely why we'd be wise to revisit some of those books we were forced to read in school. Our more mature eyes will almost certainly see all the important stuff we missed the first time through.

The Scarlet Letter, by Nathaniel Hawthorne (New York: New American Library, 1999).

Flannery O'Connor 📖

Wise Blood

My first reading of *Wise Blood* was memorable for its unpleasantness. Our English professor assigned us to keep a journal as we read it, and though the journal most likely ended up feeding a landfill fire in those days before widespread recycling, I well remember what I wrote. I hated the book and everything about it, including the wide margins that flanked the text along each outside page edge. Something about all that white space in the context of Flannery O'Connor's story made me anxious and restless, and I recall throwing the book at the wall on more than one occasion. I truly hated it.

But a funny thing happened on my way to maturity. The book began to haunt me. I could not forget it, I could not dismiss it, and most of all, I could not resist the urge to reread it. It had obviously made an impact on me, and I was determined to figure out why. Almost thirty years later, I'm not sure I've figured it out. But I do know this: *Wise Blood* is much better the second or third time around. I suspect my initial dislike was due in part to the book's depiction of the seedy side of a bleak southern city, and I'd seen enough of that in real life. I also had this nagging suspicion that I could have been related to the protagonist, Hazel Motes — not because he went around preaching the doctrines of his Church Without Christ, but because I harbored this great fear that I was surely on a path that was leading me to become just as crazy and sacrilegious and, well, seedy as he was. Like him I'd end up surrounded by a cast of dismal and eccentric characters (including, in Motes's case, the young zoo worker Enoch, whose daddy's "wise blood" coursed through his veins).

My path led me elsewhere, thank the good Lord. But back to Hazel Motes: a one-time fundamentalist who's the grandson-of-a-preacher-man, Motes is hell-bent on challenging the notion that there's any redeeming value to faith in Christ or even to life itself. Through much of the book, he "believed in blasphemy as the way to salvation, but...you couldn't even believe in that because then you were believing in something to blaspheme" (p. 206). The harder he tried to deny Jesus, the harder it became for him — right up to the last chapter, the contents of which you'll have to read for yourself. No spoilers here. Let's just say that the ending is both chilling and redemptive.

Be prepared to hate this book. But if it starts to haunt you, give it another try.

Wise Blood, by Flannery O'Connor (New York: Farrar, Straus and Giroux, 1979 edition).

Robert Penn Warren

All the King's Men

All the King's Men is ostensibly about a character named Willie Stark, a corrupt politician based loosely on Huey Long, who was governor of Louisiana from the 1920s to the early 1930s. It's told from the first-person point of view of journalist Jack Burden, who goes to work for Stark and gets caught up in his web of corruption, and it's as much about Burden as it is about Stark. An obvious moral theme runs through the novel, but that's not what made the greatest impact on me, as far as I can tell.

What struck me most was the exquisite language and imagery Robert Penn Warren, a poet, used in telling such a
gritty story. A strong sense of the eternal permeated the
author's descriptions of the physical world, and it was
that sense that kept me turning the pages.

Only as an afterthought did I realize, back in my pre-
Christian days, that I had no moral framework with
which to judge Stark's character. Like Huey Long, Stark
was a champion of the poor, and also like Long, he used
his power as governor to manipulate the system and
break the law at times in order to implement projects and
programs that benefited the poor. At the time we read
this in class, the issue of poverty was a primary social
concern — second only to Vietnam — and moral questions related to the poor dominated our discussion about
the book. The consensus was that as long as the form of
corruption — say, kickbacks from contractors bidding on
urban housing projects — didn't hurt anyone, then the
legalities were of secondary importance.

That didn't make sense to me. I mean, wrong is
wrong, right? But I had no basis from which to argue
that point. I suddenly understood the implications of the
lack of an identifiable and articulated moral standard. Today, that sounds to me like a no-brainer. But this was
more than thirty years ago, and I had just barely crossed
the threshold into adulthood. *All the King's Men* pushed
me into a more mature and complex way of thinking

about good and evil. I ended the semester with less certainty and far more questions about right and wrong than I'd ever entertained before. The questions troubled me, but Warren's poetic images sustained me. Long after I'd forgotten about the dilemma Willie Stark posed, I still remembered those images.

All the King's Men, by Robert Penn Warren (New York: Harcourt, 2001).

Bob Dylan

Just typing his name exasperates me these days. Bring him up in a conversation with me, and I guarantee I'll take a deep breath and visibly brace myself for an exercise in futility: trying to explain Bob Dylan's spirituality to label-mongers. Their opinions go something like this: "Well, I know he got saved, but then he renounced Christianity and went back to Judaism!" No, no, no. He was singing and writing about Jesus long before his publicized conversion in 1979. And he has continued to sing and write about Jesus ever since. He is a true prepostmodern, possibly the most prophetic of the lot.

The bottom line is this: Dylan's expression of faith cannot be reduced to a handy label or a one-line prayer for salvation. His is an enormous expression of faith, one that encompasses not only his Jewish and Christian beliefs but also every aspect of his life and relationship with

God. He cannot be pigeonholed into a narrow definition of Christianity according to the cultural standards of the American evangelical church, a church that remains convinced he's a spiritual goner. The playlists from any of his recent concerts indicate that he continues to sing gospel songs, hymns, and spirituals. And Dylan never sings words that he does not believe.

These days, I tend to refer Dylan-bashers to Scott Marshall, the Dylan expert with whom I wrote *Restless Pilgrim: The Spiritual Journey of Bob Dylan*. Or, if I'm feeling generous, I just hand them a copy of the book. In response to a question about his beliefs, Dylan once said, "It's all there in the lyrics." I now have my own response to the same question about him: "It's all there in the book."

Lyrics, 1962–1985, by Bob Dylan (New York: Alfred A. Knopf, 1985).

📖 Bruce Cockburn

How and where I first heard about Canadian singer/songwriter Bruce Cockburn way back in the early 1970s, I have no idea. But while my contemporaries were singing the praises of that *other* Bruce — the one "Born in the USA" — I was scouring record stores in Greenwich Village that specialized in rare and foreign recordings, in the often elusive hope of finding even one gem by this brilliant lyricist. I unearthed one or two, but by the end of the decade Cockburn had released something like ten albums, eight of which I had never heard. So I did the only thing I knew to do back in those pre-Internet days: I drove to Canada and bought them there. So maybe I was going to Canada anyway, but still, the prospect of finding *Circles in the Stream* or *Dancing in the Dragon's Jaw* was a prime motivating factor in my decision about where to go on vacation that year.

Only a few Cockburn songs have ever had significant airplay in nonurban areas in the States; "Wondering Where the Lions Are" and "Rocket Launcher" are about the best known. But they are hardly representative of Cockburn's masterful artistry as a poet and musician. His "Lord of the Starfields" alone is a magnificent psalm that beautifully expresses the haunting depth of his awe of God. Years later, that one song kept me from losing my marbles when I wasn't at church, where we held hands and swayed and sang little ditties about how we loved each other with the love of the Lord and all that. Oh, and you might want to know that the ever-passionate Cockburn occasionally uses what we euphemistically call "strong language." But only occasionally. Honest. Try *Rumours of Glory, Resumé*, or another of his compilation CDs if you're not familiar with his work.

Anything, Anytime, Anywhere, by Bruce Cockburn (Van Nuys, CA: Alfred Publishing, 2002).

Two

REBELLION, REVOLUTION, AND RELIGION

Black Power, Social Justice, and Questions about God

Somewhere in a box in the garage is my college transcript, bearing the letter grade I earned in the one creative writing class I took. That grade is one reason why I haven't looked at the transcript in decades. It's not that I received a poor grade and don't want to be reminded of that. The truth is, I have no idea what my grade was. This I do know: I faked my way through the class. I had no interest in writing and no talent for it. Or so I thought, because creative writing to me meant fiction and short stories and poetry. Creative nonfiction? Never heard of it.

At the same time, I realized that the books I read on my own — those that weren't course requirements — were all nonfiction. Most of them related to social issues, psychology, and current events; many were biographies;

and some even focused on religion, of all things. No way could I have predicted, though, that I was inching my way toward a career in journalism — and religion news writing in particular. I was going to be an English teacher! When my professor in a "teaching high school English" class suggested I consider a career as a writer, I was floored but later figured he was subtly trying to discourage me from becoming a teacher. Maybe he was; I did become a writer, and I can't help but think that the books that follow had a hand in leading me in that direction. The authors and their works also helped raise my social consciousness, another characteristic of postmodern thinking.

Malcolm X and Alex Haley
The Autobiography of Malcolm X

From the first time I heard the name Malcolm X and for years afterward, his very name, so loaded as it was with that inscrutable, big, stand-alone X, sent shivers up and down my spine. He was a revolutionary! He was a Black Muslim! He was a member of the Nation of Islam! For crying out loud, the Nation of Islam thought he was so evil, even *they* kicked him out! He wanted blacks to secede from the United States and create their own country! At least, that's how simplistic it all seemed to a white teenager who had met only one or two black people until entering tenth grade, when buses brought several dozen black students from South Jersey's rural "sending districts" to the regional high school.

And then I read *The Autobiography of Malcolm X* sometime after I entered college in 1968, three years after the assassination of Malcolm X and less than six months after the assassination of Martin Luther King Jr. Suddenly, my world expanded. I had lived out most of the events of the civil rights movement in the confines of a small, primarily white town. What I knew of the black effort I knew from television news, a mainstay in our house at 6 p.m. sharp, no matter what else was going on in our lives. I entered the larger world of college, with its more culturally diverse student body, as the combined forces of the civil rights movement and Vietnam protests gave rise to the growing movement for black power. What had frightened me as a high school student now became personal, as I got to know blacks personally — including many a Black Muslim! — and began reading the books they considered important and foundational to their way of thinking. *The Autobiography of Malcolm X* generally topped the list.

The book was not only an eye-opener but also a wonderfully written, eminently readable work that made this English major very happy indeed. I'd expected a diatribe, but what I got was so much more. I discovered that you don't have to agree with everything a person believes to come away with a respect for those beliefs and a newfound appreciation for the process that led to that particular belief system. In the final years of his life, Malcolm X abandoned many of his more radical beliefs, largely due to his discovery on a pilgrimage to Mecca that the Islam of Elijah Muhammad's Nation of Islam bore little resemblance to the real thing. But still, I struggled at the time with his blanket assessment of Christianity as an oppressive religion — and still do. But I hardly identified with Christianity at the time, and today I realize that God used this Muslim to change my perspective on the civil rights struggle by allowing me to enter the world of an oppressed black man, if only through the printed word. But what a printed word it is. Well worth reading, even a second or third time through.

The Autobiography of Malcolm X, by Malcolm X with Alex Haley (New York: Grove Press, 1965).

James Baldwin 📖

Nobody Knows My Name

Nobody Knows My Name also played a significant role in changing my thinking about people with a cause and the way they write about that cause. What — or perhaps more accurately, who — had left me with the impression that people striving for basic human rights were so myopically militant, so fanatically focused, so . . . undeniably unpleasant? It's too late and too pointless to try to find the answer to that now. Reading James Baldwin offered me another opportunity to erase those timeworn racist tapes that had been playing in my head for years.

James Baldwin was a persuasive writer who knew that all the abstract questions about race relations were meaningless and crumbled to dust when a single, cut-to-the-chase, let's-get-real question was finally posed to a white person in 1950s America, a question like this one: Would you let your sister marry a Negro? By the 1970s, when I read this book, I knew what my answer would be: I have absolutely no control over my recalcitrant sister. But that's not the point. The point to me was, Why would anyone even think of asking that question in 1970s America? Today, I'd be quick to point out that Baldwin, like so many male and even female writers and speakers, regardless of color, asked that question of only one segment of society: white men. He completely disregarded white women.

Even back then, Baldwin seemed dated to me, but I was admittedly naïve. As astonished as I was each time I noticed someone recoil at the sight of a mixed-race couple, I had to admit the recoilers were in the majority. I didn't understand it. I still don't.

Nobody Knows My Name, like *Notes of a Native Son,* is a collection of essays that either started out as magazine articles or talks given in a variety of settings. Baldwin's fiction is also compelling, at least the books I read: *Tell Me How Long the Train's Been Gone* and *Another Country.*

Ironically, Baldwin turned bitter against his Christian upbringing, even though he once preached the gospel as a child. His writings are steeped in the language of the Old Testament prophets and the only New Testament prophet of note, Jesus himself. For Baldwin to deny the power of the word of God seems disingenuous to me today.

In any event, he was undeniably a powerful and skilled writer and one very determined man. "Well, I had said that I was going to be a writer, God, Satan, and the state of Mississippi notwithstanding, and that color did not matter, and that I was going to be free," he wrote in the introduction. Later, he added, "The question of color takes up much space in these pages, but the question of color...operates to hide the graver questions of the self.... The connection between American whites and blacks is far deeper and more passionate than any of us like to think" (p. xiii). Baldwin used the word "American" intentionally and with a pointedness that his audience at the time could not have missed. Having just spent seven years or so in Europe, where the color of his skin was barely noticed, Baldwin had once again come face-to-face with the particularly American brand of racism.

Apparently, his later writings became more strident and less eloquent, but by then I had moved on to other reading obsessions, so I wouldn't know. Didn't seem like I should revisit his work, given that fairly universal assessment.

Nobody Knows My Name, by James Baldwin (New York: Dial Press, 1961).

📖 *Introduction to Sociology*

Okay, so I'm guessing at the exact title of this textbook, the required text for the Introduction to Sociology course at Monmouth College in 1971 or so. It was an oversized paperback with a yellow cover, and I reread parts of it long after I graduated, right up to the day in 1978 when it was lost to a flooded basement as I was moving in to a new and abominably defective house.

That book was one of the treasures of my college years. It so changed my way of thinking about the world that I considered switching my major from English to sociology. Fortunately for those who would have been subjected to my woefully inadequate skills as a social worker, somewhere along the line I thought about roaches and rats, shuddered for days, and in a New York ghetto heartbeat gave up on my fleeting calling. But I've never lived far from those I presumably would have helped, and that textbook opened my eyes to the myriad factors that contribute to poverty, unemployment, underemployment — and welfare abuse. So with my eyes opened to both sides of the problem, I began to see the poor in much the way I believe Jesus did — as a segment of society that may "always be with us," but whose lives can be improved and empowered.

Several years after college, I tried to talk to one of my pastors about a single mother in our church who needed help. He gave me the usual "you can give a man a fish and feed him for a day, or you can teach a man to fish and feed him for a lifetime" speech. Sexist language aside, that adage does contain a kernel of truth. But these days, teaching a man, or anyone else, to fish well enough to make a living at it takes a heck of a lot longer than a day, and the person has to eat in the meantime. I held my tongue from asking what our church was doing to teach this man — um, woman — to fish. I'd love to go back today and let my tongue loose.

Some churches continue to teach that all anyone needs is the Lord. That's fine, but honestly, I just don't see that in the teachings of Jesus. To their credit, every evangelical church I've ever been involved with has maintained a food pantry and a clothing closet to distribute much-needed goods to the poor. But that's where ministry to the poor began — within the church, distributing food and clothes to members or at least attenders — and that's pretty much where it ended. There was a serious disconnect between what I had learned in my sociology textbook and what I was seeing in the church. And then I discovered a whole other segment of the church, one that included the likes of Jim Wallis (editor of *Sojourners* and author of the recent and excellent *God's Politics: Why the Right Gets It Wrong and the Left Doesn't Get It*) and Ronald Sider (*Rich Christians in an Age of Hunger* and others). All of their books are worth reading.

Introduction to Sociology. Anyone who can identify the book I described, and can tell me how to get copy, will receive my eternal gratitude.

📖 Martin Luther King Jr.
"I've Been to the Mountaintop"

I don't recall today in what form or what publication I first read Martin Luther King's final speech. I'm not even sure I knew it was his final speech when I first read it; I suspect it was one of many speeches and essays by black leaders that I read back in the 1970s, so the words, rather than the dates and contexts, would have been far more important to me at the time. What I do know is that his words stirred up something inside my questioning soul that helped prepare me for the spiritual awakening that was several years in my future.

I know this, too: King's words in this speech, as racially focused as they were, came to reside in me as words outside the color wheel. I experienced a lot of "What???" moments as I read it, such as when King said this to God: "If you allow me to live just a few years in the second half of the twentieth century, I will be happy" (p. 209). Good grief! I didn't even want to be alive then, and I wasn't persecuted or oppressed or demeaned by anyone but my own sorry self! I loved his response to Bull Connor turning fire hoses on civil rights marchers in Birmingham. "He knew a kind of physics that didn't relate to the transphysics we knew about...we knew water. That couldn't stop us" (p. 212), King said, alluding to the waters of baptism. "Yess!!!" I thought, momentarily forgetting my disdain for religious ritual.

Then there's the final paragraph of the speech, the one that most everybody knows, and one that I hope I never tire of hearing. It's the paragraph from which the speech gets its title. King has been to the mountaintop and has seen the Promised Land, which he surely knew meant that he possessed the Promised Land, as the biblical writers professed. "I may not get there with you...I'm not worried about anything. I'm not fearing any man." In the context of his assassination the following day, those are indeed powerful words. But honestly, I don't think I knew that when I first read it. I just knew that this man had given life and voice to something deep inside me, and I wanted him to teach me more. I recall turning my attention to the God I didn't believe in, wondering how he could have let this man die when there was still so much work to be done.

A Call to Conscience: The Landmark Speeches of Dr. Martin Luther King, Jr., ed. Clayborne Carson and Kris Shepard (New York: Time Warner, 2001).

📖 Eldridge Cleaver

Soul on Ice

I am as certain as I can be that Eldridge Cleaver's *Soul on Ice* marked my introduction to Thomas Merton. That's right — Thomas Merton. Who would have thought it? Who would have thought that reading a book by one of the most militant militants of that time would serve as an introduction to one of the most monastic monastics of that time? But there he was, Thomas Merton, whose work Cleaver had read while he was doing time at San Quentin, which Cleaver considered to be an involuntary monastery. He thought Merton was nuts to pursue solitude and "incarceration," until he actually read *The Seven Storey Mountain.*

Like his hero Malcolm X, Cleaver was a one-time Black Muslim who later renounced the teachings of Elijah Muhammad. That made me happy, as did his respect for white youth, which surprised even Cleaver himself: "If a man like Malcolm X could change and repudiate racism, if I myself and other former Muslims can change, if young whites can change, then there is hope for America," Cleaver wrote in one of the book's essays, "The White Race and Its Heroes." "It was certainly strange to find myself, while steeped in the doctrine that all whites were devils by nature, commanded by the heart to applaud and acknowledge respect for these young whites.... The sins of the fathers are visited upon the heads of the children, but only if the children continue in the evil deeds of the fathers" (p. 84).

I recall feeling so validated when I read that, though I wouldn't have used that word at the time. I was fresh off a run-in with a black racist at the Port Authority bus terminal in New York City, and I was still shaken by the incident. It was one of those no-win situations, where anything I might have said would have sounded either defensive or condescending. I'd been jostled by several people as I entered one of the waiting rooms, and apparently I in turn jostled someone else. "Someone else" waited until he was clear across the room, then turned, pointed, and thundered at me, "You could at least say 'I'm sorry!'" and continued with a mini tirade on how just because I was white that didn't give me the right to push a black man around. Never mind that I weighed roughly 105 and he was at least 250. I looked all around to see who he could be talking to before I realized I was the only white girl standing in the direct line of his pointing finger. No one in the entire people-filled room made a sound. I recall looking at him, my eyes pleading with him to understand that *I was on his side!*

I muttered an apology, of course, turned bright red, and quickly changed my travel plans, which had been somewhat vagabondish to begin with. It later occurred to me — yes, I was rather dense in those days — that we're all just people, some good, some bad, some racist, some

not. But during my recovery from that highly public be-
rating and humiliation, Cleaver gave me reason to hope
that we could see genuine racial change in our society
someday. I really believed that. I really, really did.

Soul on Ice, by Eldridge Cleaver (New York: McGraw-Hill,
1968).

📖 Blaise Pascal

Pensées

My copy of *Pensées,* another of the few surviving relics
of my college years, includes an introduction in which
T. S. Eliot described an "intelligent believer," which he
considered Blaise Pascal to be: "The Christian thinker
...proceeds by rejection and elimination. He finds the
world to be so-and-so; he finds its character inexplicable
by any non-religious theory; among religions he finds
Christianity, and Catholic Christianity, to account most
satisfactorily for the world and especially for the moral
world within; and thus, by what Newman calls 'powerful and concurrent' reasons, he finds himself inexorably
committed to the dogma of the Incarnation" (xii). I like
reading and rereading that whenever someone — usually me — makes me feel less than intelligent. Because
that pretty much describes how I came to faith in Christ,
minus the Catholic part and all those masculine pro-
nouns, plus the element of "mystical" experience that

Pascal and I shared at the point of our respective conversions. Which means T. S. Eliot would have considered me an intelligent believer. Or so I'd like to think.

Pensées is not a finished book but a collection of "thoughts" (*pensées* in French) on various aspects of religious life that Pascal jotted down in the last years of his life. What strikes me about this book today is the extent to which Pascal emphasized the grace of God as the only explanation for anything good that ever comes of our lives, and how utterly miserable we are — both in our emotions and in our behavior — when we reject that grace and are thus left to our own devices. Can't say I disagree with any of that, having lived with myself for lo these many years. But Pascal does seem exceedingly harsh at times, which I don't recall thinking in my first reading. I suspect at the time I thought I deserved every harsh word he wrote.

The best thing about having the exact copy of a book I used in college is all the highlighting and underlining that dates back to a time when I didn't know nothin' from nothin' — or so it often seems from a hopefully more mature perspective three decades later. But as I skim through the book today, I realize that not all that much has changed; the passages I highlighted then are passages I would probably highlight now, like this one: "Truly it is an evil to be full of faults; but it is a still greater evil to be full of them, and to be unwilling to recognize them, since that is to add the further fault of voluntary illusion" (p. 31). *A Voluntary Illusion* — what a great title for my next memoir! I think I must have been on to something when I singled out that passage.

Here's another: "It is impossible that God should ever be the end, if He is not the beginning. We lift our eyes on high, but lean upon the sand; and the earth will dissolve, and we shall fall whilst looking at the heavens" (p. 135). I must have been giving far more serious thought to the nature of God then than I am recalling today.

Despite his hammering away at sin, which is a decidedly unpopular concept in postmillennial America, Pascal — relying as he does on a blend of reason and intuition — has a great deal to say to postmoderns, especially postmoderns still transitioning from a modern paradigm.

Pascal's Pensées, by Blaise Pascal (New York: E. P. Dutton, 1958).

📖 Anne Frank
Anne Frank: The Diary of a Young Girl

Anne Frank's diary was one of the few books that actually had a memorable impact on me as a child. It was so incredibly sad; I cried real tears all the way through, since I knew the end from the beginning. Still, I hoped beyond all hope that Anne and her family would be spared. I turned each page with a sense of dread and hopefulness, knowing but trying not to know. I swear, I walked around with a lump in my throat all through seventh grade.

When I reread the book as an adult, I suddenly saw God all over it. Weird, since I didn't recall anything about God in my earlier reading. I also saw an amazing maturity in Anne, who was only a young teenager during the years when she kept her diary. "I have one outstanding trait in my character, which must strike anyone who knows me for any length of time, and that is knowledge of myself. I can watch myself and my actions, just like an outsider. The Anne of every day I can watch without prejudice, without making excuses for her, and watch what's good and what's bad about her." What did I make of passages like that when I was thirteen, just a year or two younger than Anne was when she wrote those words? I wish I had kept a diary of my own, *The Diary of a Young Girl Reading Anne Frank: The Diary of a Young Girl.*

Though the miracle I so desperately wanted to see — the miracle that Anne and the rest of her attic-mates would be saved from the Nazis — never happened, that doesn't mean supernatural intervention wasn't evident in the Franks' lives. Because not only did Otto, Anne's father, survive the Holocaust, Anne's writings also survived. It's as if God knew the world would need a reminder that some of the special people among us can still manage to find joy in the midst of unfathomable fear and hardship. "I long for freedom and fresh air, but I believe now that we have ample compensation for our privations. I realized this quite suddenly when I sat in front of the window this morning," Anne wrote after she'd been in hiding for more than a year. "When I looked outside right into the depth of Nature and God, then I was happy, really happy."

Anne Frank: The Diary of a Young Girl, by Anne Frank (New York: Bantam, 1993).

📖 Erich Fromm
The Art of Loving

Books on love, especially romantic love, generally drive me nuts. Some "couples' books" — books for Christian couples in particular — make me ill. I can't imagine any guy following the advice in those books without feeling like a complete wuss. Of course, I think women should consider those same books to be offensive and condescending, but that, apparently, is just me.

In *The Art of Loving*, Erich Fromm took a different and healthier approach, much to my relief back in the late 1960s when I bought the book after reading several other Fromm titles. Looking over the text today, I have to conclude that my coming to faith in Christ was pretty much a foregone conclusion by then. Though his is not a Christian book, Fromm, a noted psychoanalyst, gave a fair amount of space to the biblical view of love and to the love of and for the Judeo-Christian God, without a hint of condescension.

Fromm's premise was that because of our alienation from each other in American society, we have to learn to see love as an art that can be mastered both in theory and in practice. (Remember, he was writing this in the mid 1950s, when we as a society hardly knew what alienation was, compared to what we experience today.) "Two persons fall in love when they feel they have found the best object available on the market, considering the limitations of their own exchange values," he wrote of romantic love in a consumer-driven culture. "They take the intensity of the infatuation, this being 'crazy' about each other, for proof of the intensity of their love, while it may only prove the degree of their preceding loneliness" (pp. 3–4). That rang true for me in 1969, and it rings true for me today.

It was this twentieth-century psychologist, by the way, who introduced me to the writings of the early fourteenth-century mystic Meister Eckhart. (Wouldn't it be great to have a flowchart showing how one book led to three others, which led to fourteen others, which led to...a lifetime of reading? Maybe not.)

The Art of Loving: An Enquiry into the Nature of Love, by Erich Fromm (New York: Harper & Row, 1956).

Lewis Thomas

The Lives of a Cell

It's almost like the setup for a joke: What do you get when you cross a poet with a scientist? But the answer to that question is no classic punch line. The answer is

Lewis Thomas, a man composed of cells so lively that you have to wonder whether he ever had a couch-potato day. I doubt it. When you're as restless with wonder about the natural world as Thomas was, even your downtimes would be filled with reflection, insight, and still more wonder. Which is why it comes as something of a surprise to learn that the chapters of his book started out as essays for the *New England Journal of Medicine,* a publication not exactly known for contemplation or meditative thought.

The back cover of my edition of *The Lives of a Cell* highlights this pull-out quote from one of the essays: "Once you have become permanently startled, as I am, by the realization that we are a social species, you tend to keep an eye out for the pieces of evidence that this is, by and large, good for us." I doubt there's one single sentence in the entire book that not only defines the book's premise but also describes the book's author so succinctly. The man is "permanently startled" indeed.

Thomas permanently startled me. In a book on real live organisms and their interconnectedness, I hardly expected to encounter a chapter on mythical beasts such as centaurs and griffons, who along with all the rest of their ilk "are like recurrent bad dreams, and we are well rid of them. Or so we say." Neither did I expect to discover Thomas using quotes from C. S. Lewis and Julian of Norwich to connect language with cosmological physics.

Thomas did not attribute life or the universe or existence to the activity of God or a creator or an intelligent
designer of any kind, at least not as I recall. I do remember that as I continued reading, I found traces of God and
God's handiwork on most of the pages of his book. He
ended the introductory essay on this note:

> *Item.* I have been trying to think of the earth as a
> kind of organism, but it is no go. I cannot think
> of it this way. It is too big, too complex, with too
> many working parts lacking visible connections.
> The other night, driving through a hilly, wooded
> part of southern New England, I wondered about
> this. If not like an organism, what is it like, what is
> it most like? Then, satisfactorily for that moment,
> it came to me: it is most like a single cell. (p. 5)

I don't know. That sure smacks of God and intelligent
design to me.

Bear in mind that there's a lot of heavy mental lifting
amid the lyrical poetic imagery. My first time through, I
actually tried to understand the scientific terms. I recall
giving up somewhere along page 8, where Thomas wrote
about "prokaryotic cells" and "eukaryotes (e.g., motile,
ciliated cells joined to phagocytic ones)." The sound of
the word "eukaryotes" today conjures up the image of
a kind of liturgical karaoke bar at the communion rail,
which hardly enhances my understanding of the text.

From that point on, I quit trying to understand things beyond my ken. I found great pleasure in ignoring the meanings — but not the sound — of words like choloroplast and lysogeny and desquamated, delighting instead in Thomas's wit and literary prose and creative thinking. (Case in point regarding his "creative thinking": If we discover that extraterrestrials exist, he suggested sending music to establish communication with them: "I would vote for Bach, all of Bach, streamed out into space, over and over again. We would be bragging, of course, but...we can tell the harder truths later on.")

More of Thomas's wonderful essays are compiled in *The Youngest Science,* which I have read, and *The Medusa and the Snail,* which I haven't. So many books and all that.

The Lives of a Cell: Notes of a Biology Watcher, by Lewis Thomas (New York: Penguin Books, 1974).

Also Recommended

Neil Postman / *Amusing Ourselves to Death: Public Discourse in the Age of Show Business*

This is a decades-old look at the impact of television on decision making and public policy. Neil Postman was a personal favorite and a powerful influence on my decision to become a journalist.

(New York: Viking, 1985).

Edward Steichen, ed. / *The Family of Man*

I came *this* close — see that minuscule space between my thumb and index finger? — to becoming a photo-journalist thanks to this book, which was first released in 1955 and kept me entranced for hours when I was a child. It was only a serious problem with impatience that kept me from pursuing photography as a career; I found I had little tolerance for the nuances of the photo developing process. The book is a tribute to the Family of Man photography exhibit at the Museum of Modern Art and includes a commentary by Carl Sandburg. I could still spend hours with this book, if only I had them to spend.

(New York: Museum of Modern Art, 1995).

Joseph Campbell / *The Hero with a Thousand Faces*

During college, this book seriously upset my belief in the Bible as the word of God. Today, I can read it with my faith intact and appreciate Campbell's look at the common myths found in ancient cultures.

(New York: MJF Books, 1949).

Three

TRUE
SPIRITUALITY
Christian Writers and Genuine Faith

It was during my final year of college that I conceded victory to God. He just wouldn't go away. This was no fleeting encounter; he meant business with me. I became immersed not only in the waters of baptism but also in the books of myriad Christian writers. I wanted to know every single thing I could about the Bible and Jesus and Christianity.

When the shine wore off, which it always does, I found myself in this bewildering environment called church. I had attended church as a child, so it wasn't the trappings that were bewildering. It was the disconnect between the vibrant faith I had found in college and the mind-numbing reality of church life.

Today, many of us are rethinking the way we do church. Everything is back on the table. Some of what has been the norm in church services may stay, but a lot has already changed and will continue to change. One thing is certain: the traditional pastor-congregation model is gone (and all God's children said, "Amen!"). Leadership in "emerging" churches — those that are making the transition toward appealing to postmoderns — is likely to be a shared or team effort. Postmoderns need and expect to be fully involved in the life of the church, which they see as a community.

Among the many authors I read back then are some whose writings still hold up, even in the third millennium. They were postmoderns when postmodernism in the church wasn't exactly cool. They were the forerunners, the men and women — okay, the woman — who kept us sane back in the 1970s as evangelicals like me played church week after week, always sensing, always *knowing* there was more, much more. They showed us the possibility of living a spiritually rich life. They were, and are, our heroes.

Would those who have passed on consider themselves postmoderns if they were alive today? Maybe not. Were they postmodern in everything they wrote and said? Definitely not. But each one, in his or her own way, heralded the changes that were to come — the changes that are still in their infancy in these single-digit years of the twenty-first century.

Though there is likely to be some crossover, a list of influential authors among prepostmodern Catholics, Episcopalians, and liberal Protestant denominations would likely be very different from this one. Here and there, you'll find not only prepostmodern authors who were alive in the twentieth century but also an occasional writer from church history like Augustine. They all had a profound influence on me and many other Jesus freaks.

📖 Francis and Edith Schaeffer
True Spirituality

Oh, for a thousand Schaeffers to sing our great re-deemer's praise! What would the 1970s have been with-out Francis Schaeffer? How could we ever have hoped to make sense out of all the changes in the church, in the country, in the world, without him? More than any other thinker at that time, Schaeffer helped shape my own thinking and my own worldview. Which may or may not be a compliment to him, so I'll qualify that and limit his influence to my moments of lucid thinking.

Where to begin with Schaeffer is almost as difficult as deciding where to begin with C. S. Lewis. *True Spir-ituality, The God Who Is There, Escape from Reason, He Is There and He Is Not Silent*...yes, certainly all of those. *How Should We Then Live?* is another classic, as is *Whatever Happened to the Human Race?* Oh, just forget it — they're all classics. You can't go wrong if you pick up a book by Francis Schaeffer. And while you'll find him to be exceedingly modern in certain respects — his approach to faith and ministry relied largely on the use of reason and intellect to discover the truth about God — the community known as L'Abri that the Schaeffers founded in Switzerland is about as close to a postmodern church model as you're likely to find anywhere. L'Abri was a true seeker center, attracting Christians and pre-Christians who found the freedom to ask the questions so many of us were discouraged from asking in our churches. It was also one of the few places where evangelicals could find their faith expressed through the arts.

I'm including Edith Schaeffer with Francis because (1) she truly was his partner in ministry, and, to a lesser extent, in writing, and (2) I had to recognize the contributions of at least one woman of that era, even if Christian publishers didn't. I find it hard to believe that there were so few female Christian writers of substance in the '70s; I suspect they simply had a devil of a time getting published. Edith Schaeffer was certainly no intellectual lightweight, yet her best-known book, *Hidden Art,* focuses on hospitality and home-oriented topics. That says more about the biases of Christian publishers back then than it does about her contribution to the Christian world, which was far more significant than that book implies. She wrote other books, but *Hidden Art* seems to have been the best marketed, and it's one of the few you can still find in print.

True Spirituality, by Francis A. Schaeffer (Wheaton, IL: Tyndale House, 1971).

📖 Svetlana Alliluyeva

Only One Year

When her father died in 1953, Svetlana, a twenty-seven-year-old Russian woman decided it was time to change her last name to honor her mother, Nadezhda Alliluyeva, who had supposedly died of peritonitis when Svetlana was only six. Not such a surprising move, considering Svetlana's father was Joseph Stalin, and her mother's intestinal disease more closely resembled suicide — or murder. Either way, anyone with a brain figured Stalin was to blame, given his penchant for offing every person who crossed him and even some who didn't. A wife didn't stand a chance.

In 1967, Stalin's female spawn defected to the U.S., which prompted a whole lot of Commie haters to say "I told you so." The Soviets then forced a change in the U.S. policy toward Soviet defectors, who thereafter would need to be debriefed by the Soviets before being granted asylum. This after Alliluyeva denounced both her father's regime and the then current Soviet government headed by Andrei Kosygin (remember him?).

Alliluyeva's story so intrigued me that I bought her autobiography in hardback, no mean feat for a starving student in 1972. Well, I wasn't exactly starving, because students qualified for food stamps — a sure sign, some said, that we were headed toward becoming a socialist state. Perfect timing, really.

It's not the best-written book in the world — and it is, after all, a translation, which adds yet another hand to the mix — but I didn't care about that then, and I doubt that it would bother me much today. Alliluyeva's story is a powerful testimony to the faithfulness of God, a God so faithful that he would not allow the atheism her father drilled into her to take root in her life. Instead, the religious sensitivity her grandmothers instilled in her beat the tar out of Stalin's materialistic philosophy.

"Until I experienced [faith] myself, I knew not that I had it, just as a man cannot know he has a musical ear until he has heard a melody," she wrote. "The melody of a religious feeling is the music of life itself. To those who do not hear it I could not explain what it sounds like.... If the spark isn't smoldering inside one, no efforts can ever bring it into existence. Water cannot catch fire. But if there is a smoldering within one's heart, then sooner or later, under certain conditions, it is bound to burst into bright flame. That, in all probability, is what happened to me" (p. 293).

I don't know about her theory regarding that missing spark — God might be inclined to remind her about a certain Elijah and the prophets of Baal and a pool of water that caught fire — but her conversion story remains a dramatic one. It so amazed me that I completely forgot to feel smug about Christendom's newest celebrity convert.

Only One Year, by Svetlana Alliluyeva (New York: Harper-Collins, 1969).

📖 G. K. Chesterton

Orthodoxy

Oh my. The thoughts, the thoughts. The temptation to string together a series of G. K. Chesterton quotes and let him speak for himself is simply overwhelming. But I'll begin with this background: Chesterton wrote *Orthodoxy* in 1908 in response to criticism of one of his previous books, *Heretics*, in which he spoke out against certain popular heresies but never indicated what he himself believed. In *Orthodoxy* he described the process that led him to conclude that orthodox Christianity was the belief system and worldview that made the most sense. He eventually came to embrace the whole package, Christ and all — not just an acceptable semblance of religion.

Chesterton thoroughly enjoyed life, and the humor in *Orthodoxy* makes me want to knock back a pint of nonalcoholic brew with him in a neighborhood pub. What a delightful dinner guest he would make! Where are people like that when Domino's delivers an extra pizza by mistake? I want to hear more about a certain Mr. Batchford, whom Chesterton described as "the only early Christian who ought really to have been eaten by lions" (p. 36). And I'd love to lure him into an after-dinner squabble about men's views on women. Here's one passage he wrote: "Some stupid people started the idea that because women obviously back up their own people through everything, therefore women are blind and don't see anything. They can hardly have known any women. The same women who are ready to defend their men through thick and thin are . . . almost morbidly lucid about the thinness of his excuses or the thickness of his head" (p. 76). I do love this man's wit.

I can't help it. Here are some favorite Chestertonisms:

Christianity even when watered down is hot enough to boil all modern society to rags. (p. 125)

Christianity is a superhuman paradox where two opposite passions may blaze beside each other. (p. 154)

How can we say the Church wishes to bring us back to the Dark Ages? The Church was the only thing that ever brought us out of them. (p. 154)

We die daily. We are always being born again with almost indecent obstetrics. (p. 156)

A clergyman may be apparently as useless as a cat, but he is also as fascinating, for there must be some strange reason for his existence. (p. 163)

It did for one wild moment cross my mind that, perhaps, those might not be the very best judges of the relation of religion to happiness who, by their own account, had neither one nor the other. (p. 92)

I'll stop, but not willingly. I wouldn't want to leave the impression that *Orthodoxy* is a compendium of one-liners. It isn't; it's a thoughtful, logical, well-reasoned-out coming-to-faith story, told by a joyful literary giant.

Orthodoxy, by G. K. Chesterton (San Francisco: Ignatius, 1995).

📖 C. S. Lewis

Mere Christianity

Let me state this up front: C. S. Lewis is my favorite Christian writer. I could go for months on a single sentence from Lewis's pen; there's no telling how long I could last if I were stranded on a desert island with nothing but the collected works of C. S. Lewis for company. *Mere Christianity* tops my list of "the best of Lewis," if only because it's arguably the definitive presentation of the gospel published in the twentieth century. But I also have to give a major nod to the Chronicles of Narnia series as well as the series commonly referred to as the space trilogy — the only, and I emphasize *only,* fantasy and science fiction books I ever enjoyed reading until J. K. Rowling came along.

Because Lewis was a genius, and because he wrote so many "important" books, many people seem to have forgotten that a great deal of his appeal can be attributed to his incomparable wit. For an academic who inhabited the hallowed halls of Oxford and Cambridge, Lewis proved himself to be anything but a stuffy scholar. His sophisticated wit helped many of us retain our sense of humor even as our pastors were thundering at us from the pulpit about our weighty responsibility to personally usher in the Kingdom of God.

Lewis was a prolific writer — a mixed blessing that makes it tough for me to narrow down the list of Lewis must-reads. *The Screwtape Letters*, for sure. *The Problem of Pain* and *Surprised by Joy* — yes. Then what? *Miracles, The Great Divorce, The Pilgrim's Regress, The Case for Christianity?* How about Lewis's personal favorite, *Till We Have Faces?* Oh, the choices, the choices! It's much too difficult for me to bear. Just read them all, everything Lewis wrote after he came to faith in Christ. His pre-Christian stuff is probably just as good, but there are only so many reading hours in a lifetime, and with Lewis, you have to draw the line somewhere. Because you'll probably want to reread some of his books, whenever you need another Lewis fix.

Mere Christianity, by C. S. Lewis (New York: Macmillan, 1952).

Oswald Chambers
My Utmost for His Highest

There is one book of devotional readings I've kept in constant use for nearly thirty years now: *My Utmost for His Highest*. I've never felt even the slightest urge to replace it with the updated version. The problem with Oswald Chambers for many people is not his antiquated language but his unapologetic allegiance to biblical truth. He was the kind of guy who could smack the truth across your face with such grace that you'd end up thanking him for the pain he inflicted. He had no patience with preachers — or any professing believer, for that matter — who didn't speak directly and clearly about the things of God. Don't talk about your faith; talk about your God! Don't call them your shortcomings; call them your sins! Don't put God in first place in your life; put him in *every* place in your life! Somehow, his directness made him all the more endearing. My guess is that's partly because he actually lived what he preached.

So how does this forthright Bible literalist fit into a postmodern theology? Just look at this one nugget, my all-time favorite quote of his: "Never make a principle out of your experience; let God be as original with other people as He is with you" (p. 165). I have no doubt that my beloved Mr. Chambers could have single-handedly put an end to the malarkey in recent decades that saw one ministry after another set itself up as the only true expression of faith — often based on some unremarkable principle the pastor had "discovered" through an experience. And we were all expected to fall in line behind this one man's version of the church, regardless of the unique ways God wanted to use us in ministry. No thanks. I prefer a stinging, honest rebuke from a genuinely godly person who allows me to be me.

My Utmost for His Highest, by Oswald Chambers (Copyright 1993 by Oswald Chambers Publications Association, Ltd. Original edition copyright 1935 by Dodd, Mead & Company, New York. Copyright renewed 1963 by Oswald Chambers Publications Association, Ltd.).

Andrew Murray 📖

With Christ in the School of Prayer

Somewhere in a landfill or thrift store or maybe even in a carton in my very own garage is my cherished copy of Andrew Murray's classic book on prayer, *With Christ in the School of Prayer*, which if I'm not mistaken is the first book I read after I came to faith in Christ. Prayer did not come easily to me then; I felt as if I was talking to myself, which I'd already been doing for years. Prayer, I figured, should be something special and not just more of the same. I can't say I was learning much by listening to how other people prayed, especially at the Wednesday night prayer meeting at the Baptist church I attended. There, the crowd of mostly older women specialized in "unspoken requests," and that just taught me to shut up.

Murray immediately put to rest one of my already entrenched misconceptions about prayer, right in the preface: "As long as we look on prayer chiefly as the means of maintaining our own Christian life, we shall not know fully what it is meant to be." No question about it — prayer, to me, was a maintenance discipline, something I had to do to keep my status as a Christian intact, like going to church at precisely 11 a.m. every Sunday and reading the Bible all the way through every year, year after biblical year.

Murray continued: "When we learn to regard [prayer] as the highest part of the work entrusted to us, the root and strength of all other work, we shall see that there is nothing that we so need to study and practise as the art of praying aright." Study? Practise — or practice, as we say in the colonies? "Praying aright"? I had no problem believing my prayers could be inferior or inadequate or ineffective, but was it possible I was praying "awrong"?

Murray's legalistic tone aside — which softens later — his "instruction" on prayer, with Jesus as the teacher, actually did help me get over my shyness about praying in public and my uncertainty that the prayers I prayed in private really were heard by someone other than just me. Looking over the text today, which like many other classics is available on the Christian Classics Ethereal Library at *www.ccel.org,* I marvel at how comfortable I was back in the 1970s with the KJV language Murray used in his own writing. I guess we were all so used to the King James Bible that we were undaunted by sixteenth-century style when we encountered it in the twentieth.

Murray's book has been updated to appeal to contemporary readers, which is probably a good thing. But I'll always root first for the original; if you're not put off by the language, you won't find a better or more thorough book on prayer.

With Christ in the School of Prayer, by Andrew Murray (Christian Classics Ethereal Library, *www.ccel.org*).

Thomas à Kempis 📖
The Imitation of Christ

One of my most faithful and constant companions in my early years as a Christian was this priceless guide to spiritual devotion, written by a fifteenth-century German monk. (Is it any wonder I was drawn to the monastic life? I was thoroughly Baptist, but my reading list was peppered with writings by monks.) I was surprised in later years to learn that Thomas à Kempis was writing for his monastic community; I assumed he was writing for the Christian community at large. I've heard that *The Imitation of Christ* was the second-best-selling book in history after the Bible; I'm not sure if this is still true, but either way a lot of people have read this book and apparently agree that it's well worth reading.

To this day, I enjoy leafing through the book and skimming the chapter subtitles: "What the Truth Saith Inwardly without Noise of Words" (chapter 2 of the third book; the complete volume consists of four books) and "Of Avoiding Curious Inquiry into the Life of Another"

(chapter 24, third book) and "Of the Danger of Super-
fluity of Words" (chapter 10, first book). Thomas covered
a lot of ground in relatively few pages. His premise is
evident in the title — our lives need to be conformed to
the kind of life Christ lived — but he applied that imitation or conformity to specific areas of thought, word,
and deed.

Contemporary sensibilities may provoke some read-
ers to bristle at some of Thomas's assertions ("That Man
Hath No Good in Himself, and Nothing Whereof to
Glory," chapter 4, third book), but just skip around and
you'll eventually stumble on a more grace-filled section
("That a Man Must Not Be Too Much Cast Down When
He Falleth into Some Faults," chapter 57, third book).
That's one of the great features of *The Imitation of Christ;*
most of it is written in a way that allows you to open to
any page and begin reading — slowly and meditatively, to
get the full benefit of Thomas's spiritual wisdom. Even
those portions that seem harsh, particularly those that
place human nature and the secular world in a negative
light, are balanced out by Thomas's reflections on God's
grace and forgiveness.

In some respects, Thomas is a man for the third millennium. He had a certain amount of disdain for book
knowledge, or rather book knowledge at the expense of
a Christlike character — ironic, considering the popular-
ity his own book has enjoyed for five hundred years or
so. All his talk about the pointlessness of books and their

authors, though, doesn't exactly cheer me, especially at the moment. "Of a surety, at the Day of Judgment it will be demanded of us, not what we have read, but what we have done." Uh-oh.

The Imitation of Christ, by Thomas à Kempis (Westwood, NJ: Christian Library, 1984, and a contemporary translation by William Griffin copyright 2000 published by HarperSanFrancisco).

The Confessions of St. Augustine

If it's true that youth is wasted on the young, then I say it's equally true that college is wasted on the young. I propose that we change our way of thinking about college by training young people for a job and giving them a fully funded sabbatical from those jobs so they can acquire a well-rounded education later on, when they're ready and maybe even eager for it. Okay, so maybe I'm just preaching to and about myself, but still, it's a good idea.

Which brings me to Augustine, who had a good idea along about the year 397. That's when he started writing his *Confessions,* considered by scholars who know this sort of thing to be the first real autobiography. I didn't appreciate that good idea circa 1969, when I read excerpts of the book in a world literature course. Looking back on it now, I wonder what on earth we were expected to glean from that experience. I still have the textbook we used, further proof that I seldom release my grip on a book.

Considering the lack of marginal notes, underlining, or highlighting (did we even have highlighters back then? I think not) in the Augustine section, I have to assume that I got nothing out of it.

It wasn't until I became a Christian and began hearing more about Augustine that I decided to give *Confessions* another try, this time in a more appealing translation than the one I encountered in college. Expecting to find a dense historical document — I suppose I was attracted to dense historical documents at the time — I was astonished at Augustine's candor about his life, particularly his sexual life, and the authenticity of his writing. Not only was his the first autobiography, it was also the first tell-all in publishing history! The man held nothing back, and his vulnerability and openness nudged me toward becoming more candid about my own life. The difference between Augustine and other tell-all authors was evident: his telling of all served a larger purpose, functioning as it did as a springboard for a theological grappling with sin and temptation and as a window into the mind of a fully alive, fully engaged, worldly man whose life had been genuinely transformed through an encounter with the living God.

All that was wasted on me in 1969; Augustine's brilliance was lost amid the brilliance of so many other classical writers we studied that year. Or maybe it was just the translation. I'm sure there are many good ones out there, but of the two I've read, Rex Warner's is clearly the winner. Augustine's relevance to contemporary readers, specifically Christian readers, is made even clearer by Warner's hand.

The Confessions of St. Augustine, trans. Rex Warner (New York: Penguin/Mentor, 1963).

Dietrich Bonhoeffer 📖

The Cost of Discipleship

German theologian Dietrich Bonhoeffer died long before the 1970s, executed by the Nazis in a concentration camp a month or so before Hitler committed suicide and Germany surrendered in 1945. One of a few professing Christians who gave their lives opposing Hitler's regime, Bonhoeffer had two significant strikes against him: he helped a small group of Jews escape from Germany into Switzerland, and he participated in a plot to assassinate Hitler — a bit of a blot on his reputation as a pacifist. (A side note here: While Christians have hailed him for his courage in identifying with the doomed Jews, some Jews point out that he actually died for the cause of the church, which Hitler was intent on demolishing. Either way, the fact remains that Bonhoeffer was a martyr.)

Like many others who came to faith through the Jesus People Movement, I read Bonhoeffer's *The Cost of Discipleship* so many times that pretty much every sentence in the book ended up underlined. It later fell victim to a flood in my basement as a late-winter downpour forced melted ice and snow through the casement windows and right on top of several cartons of books. So many treasures were lost in that flood that I moved right out, a mere two months after I had rented the place.

Back to Bonhoeffer. Though he worked mostly in a traditional church setting, Bonhoeffer's views of the *ecclesia,* or the necessity of communal faith in the life of a believer, would ring true with most postmoderns. And he should be lauded by postmoderns and all thinking Christians for no other reason than for giving us the phrase "cheap grace." Sixty years after his death, way too many church leaders, in America anyway, are still dishing out the totally unbiblical and unrealistic idea that you can come to Christ without actually becoming a *disciple* of Christ. In their version of grace, you can get all the benefits without the nuisance of sacrificial living and obedience to God at all costs, especially if you respond in the next ten minutes. The spiritual landscape is strewn with the souls of unsuspecting seekers who believed the lie and walked away from God when they discovered that the Christian life wasn't all it was cracked up to be.

The Cost of Discipleship, by Dietrich Bonhoeffer (London: SCM Press, 1959, published in the U.S. by Simon & Schuster, first Touchstone Edition 1995).

Brother Lawrence

The Practice of the Presence of God

My friend Gail, to whom I owe actual money as well as a priceless debt, disappeared from my radar screen nearly thirty years ago but left a legacy that I can only hope to leave in someone else's life. Gail was the first person I knew as an adult who had a brain, a personality, and a sense of humor and also believed that Jesus rose from the dead and was the son of God and had something to say to her life in the early 1970s. This was off-the-charts faith and maybe off-the-wall thinking. But she lived a life that was consistent with that faith, and she was the catalyst that led me to that final no-turning-back decision to dedicate my life to God.

Introducing me to a life with God was plenty for one person to accomplish. Really, if she hadn't done another thing for me for the rest of my life, I'm fairly sure that would have been enough. But no. Gail compounded my debt to her by introducing me to Andrew Murray and to Brother Lawrence, a seventeenth-century lay brother in a Carmelite monastery.

It's only because of a fluke that Brother Lawrence's name means anything to us today. Assigned to a monastery kitchen, where he worked for nearly forty years, Brother Lawrence happened to become involved in a conversation with a Catholic Church official who recognized the depth of his spiritual wisdom and understanding. Over the years they wrote to each other, and it's that correspondence that resulted in *The Practice of the Presence of God*, a classic work on developing a constant awareness of God's presence in all of life. In creating this consciousness of the ever-present God, Brother Lawrence wrote, we bring a sacredness to all that we do, no matter how menial or mundane the task. To Brother Lawrence's way of thinking, there's no distinction between secular and religious work or secular and religious life. In our conscious awareness of God, all our thoughts become prayers to him.

The result in Lawrence's life was a tranquility that few of us have any hope of achieving. The result in my life was a constant awareness of God, though sometimes it's his absence I feel more than his presence. And instead of making me consistently serene and joyful, an unbroken awareness of the presence of God has often made me neurotic and perfectionistic instead. I think I missed the section of the book that clearly defined God's presence as God's *loving* presence. Either that or somewhere along the line Brother Lawrence's words got lost amid a barrage of rules about how to really live the Christian life. I think I'm finally on the road to maturity, though, because God's presence hasn't fed my neurosis in a fairly long time.

The Practice of the Presence of God, by Brother Lawrence (New Kensington, PA: Whitaker House, 1982).

A. W. Tozer 📖

The Pursuit of God

Another critic of complacency, A. W. Tozer had a remarkable gift as an author: his words manage to sound fresh no matter how many times you reread them. I suspect that's because his entire being was wrapped up in a quest for the deeper things of God. *The Pursuit of God* in particular is a classic; the underlined passages in my copy *still* speak to me in a profound and intense way, some thirty years after I first bought the book. *The Divine Conquest* and *Man: The Dwelling Place of God* are also considered classics. Tozer wrote a dozen books, and several dozen more have been created from his notes and sermons. I doubt that there's a shallow or superficial thought in any of them.

One of the things I love about Tozer, besides his delightful name, is the way he beat the odds without ever trying to. He not only had no formal theological training, but he had very little education of any kind, yet by the time he was in his early thirties he was pastoring a thriving congregation in Chicago that later attracted professors and students from colleges and seminaries in the city. He also became the editor of a denominational publication. (For that reason alone he would have been one of my heroes. At the time I discovered him, journalism was quickly becoming "professionalized," a trend I abhorred. Without a communications degree, a guy like

Tozer couldn't get an interview at that same publication today.)

He was also a rarity, something of a mystic who served in a traditional Protestant church setting. Tozer advocated regular times of silence and solitude, and he believed in pursuing God with both the heart and the intellect. Better yet, he lived those precepts. I have a feeling Tozer would feel very much at home with today's emerging church types.

The Pursuit of God, by A. W. Tozer (Harrisburg, PA: Christian Publications, 1948).

Malcolm Muggeridge
Jesus: The Man Who Lives

British journalist and broadcaster Malcolm Muggeridge had little respect for C. S. Lewis, one of his contemporaries. I've never understood why that is. But he greatly admired Dietrich Bonhoeffer, so I decided to call it a draw and include him here. Besides, he was one of the few people in this chapter that I've ever been in the same room with, so he merits special attention for that reason alone. Plus he was being dogged by Francis Thompson's "Hound of Heaven" at precisely the same time I was, so his story resonates with mine. Muggeridge one-upped me, though, coming to faith as he quietly sat in the Church of the Nativity in Bethlehem rather than on the porch of a house filled with noisy college students at the Jersey Shore. But he took a major beating from the media as a result of his conversion; skeptics, especially in England, had a hard time believing that this cranky curmudgeon had experienced a genuine turnaround.

Muggeridge's *Jesus Rediscovered*, a collection of essays on religious themes that in large part predate his conversion, records the final stages of his journey toward a life of faith, while his autobiographical *Chronicles of Wasted Time* (is that a great title or what?) offers a more comprehensive look at both his life and the times he lived in. But most Muggeridge fans — those who are Christians, anyway — pretty much agree that *Jesus: The Man Who Lives* is his greatest literary achievement.

By the way, if you need someone to blame for Mother-Teresa-mania, look no further than Muggeridge. He "discovered" her and told her story to the world through a BBC documentary and subsequent book, both titled *Something Beautiful for God*. And he was one of the few people to interview Aleksandr Solzhenitsyn after the latter took his own beating from the press for expressing his opinion that Christianity offered the only hope for what ailed the West.

Jesus Rediscovered, by Malcolm Muggeridge (New York: Fontana, 1969).

📖 J. I. Packer

Knowing God

"What is the best thing in life, bringing more joy, delight, and contentment than anything else?" J. I. Packer asked. "Knowledge of God," he answered with certainty and assertiveness. People who don't know God would dispute that assertion, and even those of us who know God have our doubts from time to time. When God seems to be on everyone else's side and seems to have turned a deaf ear to our plaintive wailings, knowing God hardly seems to be a good thing, let alone the best.

But in our moments of clarity, when our stomachs are full, the bills all paid, and our immediate needs met, most of us would admit that knowing God really is the best thing in life. One thing is for sure — once you come to know God, it's awfully hard to go back and counterproductive to not go forward to get to know God better. I wish I could remember who said this or where I read it, but I fully agree with one Christian leader's opinion that "a little religion is a dangerous thing." Not only because you can get it all wrong, but also because you can miss out on the joy that comes when you get to know God more intimately.

That's when Packer's book is most helpful — when you've reached a point where you know you need a systematic study of the nature of God. I don't think this book has ever gone out of print in the thirty-plus years since its release. It really is the best book I know of for those who want to examine the theology of God, and more importantly, get better acquainted with the God they serve and love.

Even so, Packer acknowledges that there is one thing that matters more than knowing God: "What matters supremely, therefore, is not, in the last analysis, the fact that I know God, but the larger fact that underlies it — the fact that He knows me.... I am never out of His mind." Packer has written many other books, many equally good but none better than *Knowing God*.

Knowing God, by J. I. Packer (Downers Grove, IL: InterVarsity, 1973).

John Warwick Montgomery 📖
Christianity for the Tough Minded

One of the subtitles (yes, there really are two) for *Christianity for the Tough Minded* is *Essays Written by a Group of Young Scholars Who Are Totally Convinced that a Spiritual Commitment Is Intellectually Defensible,* which raises three questions: Is it any wonder my friends and I each sported a dog-eared, underlined, tattered copy of this title? Why did this group of young scholars fade into obscurity? And do we need further proof that readers had longer attention spans in the '70s, with a subtitle like that?

John Warwick Montgomery and crew took on some of my favorites at the time — Erich Hoffer, who was once called "the philosopher of the misfits," Franz Kafka, Hermann Hesse — and others I could never get into, like Ayn Rand, Herbert Marcuse, and Hugh Schonfield, whose best seller *The Passover Plot* was read by every living soul in America except me. But that didn't stop me from reading the essay that ripped him to shreds. I loved this stuff, even if I didn't always get it. I realize now that it's probably a good idea to read a book before you read an essay arguing against the premises of said book.

Montgomery went on to write and edit more books than I had time to read, but as far as his team of theological scholars is concerned, I never heard another peep out of any of them. Maybe they're all acclaimed, extensively published academic writers, but not one name rings a bell with me today. Not even Robert A. Sabath, whose essay was titled "LSD and Religious Truth," or Clark Eugene Barshinger, who wrote "Existential Psychology and Christian Faith," both heady topics at the time. Their co-contributors provided commentary on equally timely issues, like situation ethics, fundamental Buddhism, the relationship between science and faith, the theology of war, and something called the "structural-functionalist approach to religion," in which the author, one Bruce Bonecutter, mentioned two other books that were favorites of mine at the time, Desmond Morris's *Naked Ape* and Konrad Lorenz's *On*

Aggression, the '70s being my anthropology-reading era. I seem to have been determined to leave no field of study unturned, and Montgomery helped me to look at those areas of interest through the grid of faith and religion.

Christianity for the Tough Minded, ed. John Warwick Montgomery (Minneapolis: Bethany Fellowship, 1973).

Margaret Clarkson 📖
Conversations with a Barred Owl

Margaret Clarkson, a Canadian teacher and hymn writer, took up bird-watching somewhat late in life but immediately began to detect evidences of God's truth in her observations of avian behavior. *Conversations with a Barred Owl* offers a glimpse into the spiritual insights she gleaned not only from observing birds but also from talking with them. The conversations mentioned in the title were literal ones.

There's a lot in this book that would appeal only to a bird-watcher, but Clarkson's sense of wonder at the natural world sparked in me a fresh appreciation for creation. This was back in the 1970s, when the closest I came to nature was the Bronx Zoo. I'm not saying Clarkson was responsible for my subsequent transformation, but the facts don't lie: Not long after reading this book, I took up backpacking. For several years I spent every vacation on the Appalachian Trail. And yes, I did pay more attention to the morning birdsong than I ever had before.

I'm guessing that if I had the time to go back and read this book today, I'd find Clarkson's spiritual insights fairly basic. But back then I was a new Christian, and I considered pretty much everything I read about God to be infinitely profound. Glancing through the book just now, I can see where Clarkson seemed to have simply tacked on a devotional thought at the end of each essay, which would never fly, so to speak, with Christian publishers today. Still, this is one of those books from my early Christian days that I just can't seem to part with. It holds a wealth of pleasant memories for me.

Conversations with a Barred Owl: The Confession of a New Bird Watcher, by Margaret Clarkson (Grand Rapids, MI: Zondervan, 1975).

📖 Josh McDowell
Evidence That Demands a Verdict

Like a true modernist, in the 1970s I was addicted to proving, beyond a shadow of doubt, that the Bible was true! That Jesus rose from the dead! That there was incontrovertible, irrefutable, inarguable proof that every single doctrine was based on verifiable fact! Ironic, considering my spiritual journey to that point. Pre-conversion, I spent my idle hours engaged in philo-sophical debate over the meaning of life with anyone who would play the game with me. I'm sure we made no sense; what we thought were deep insights were no doubt nothing but a mass of illogical, poorly thought-out words that still hang in the air over the Inkwell in West Long Branch, New Jersey, a coffeehouse I miss today more than I should. It was the kind of place that relied on a steady stream of stoned patrons with deep philosoph-ical insights and a taste for Muenster-cheese-and-apple sandwiches on black bread.

I really believed the intellect was the seat of all that was true and important and meaningful in life. If a thing couldn't be explained by the intellect, that thing wasn't real. Even a Timothy Leary–approved experience had to have a rational explanation — even when it didn't. About the worst thing a person could call you, aside from maybe fascist pig, was anti-intellectual.

And then I had an encounter with God. One of those lightning-bolt-out-of-the-sky, bona fide, life-changing encounters, only mine involved a full moon and a calm Atlantic Ocean instead of thunder and lightning. My mind had no choice but to give way to my heart, so powerful was the experience. Just like that, I was changed, transformed in some supernatural way from a disturbed young woman whose life had spun out of control to a disturbed young woman who was loved by God and who experienced real hope for the first time in pretty much forever. I can't prove to anyone that the encounter was real. All I can do is declare what happened, and I really don't think a purely emotional experience plus a heavy dose of wishful thinking could have kept me committed to God for thirty-plus years.

So I had this supernatural experience, and what did I do next? I started to intellectualize the whole thing. I set out on a mission to prove that Christianity was true. After all, I was a Christian now, so it had better be intellectually defensible. Yet no one could ever convince me, by any argument, any scholarly debate, any academic treatise, any anything, that my encounter with God was anything less than real. That was fine for me, I guess, but I absolutely had to prove absolutely that Christianity was absolutely true to absolutely everyone I ever met. Which is where Josh McDowell finally comes in.

McDowell was the Jesus People Movement's intellectual guru, despite our horror at that four-letter Eastern-religion-and-therefore-anathema word. Like a crack attorney in a tension-filled courtroom, McDowell presented evidence, exhibits alpha through omega, that demanded a verdict of guilty as charged! In *Evidence That Demands a Verdict*, Jesus Christ was found guilty of being resurrected from the dead and fulfilling countless prophecies, thereby proving himself to be the son of God, not to mention the Way, the Truth, and the Life. On a second charge, Christianity was found to be guilty as charged! Guilty of being the one true religion. We called it One Way, and we were as happy as pigs in mud. McDowell had vindicated us. We could be Christian and still be intellectual. We had proof.

Oh, McDowell wrote a sequel, maybe in response to an appeal filed by the adversary. It was called *More Evidence That Demands a Verdict,* and at the time I didn't understand most of it since he talked about the documentary hypothesis and form criticism and all manner of theological stuff I'd never heard of at that point, given my feeble religious education. Didn't matter. I had Josh's first book, all the evidence I needed.

Evidence That Demands a Verdict, by Josh McDowell (San Bernardino, CA: Campus Crusade for Christ, 1972).

Robert Short 📖

The Gospel According to Peanuts

I still remember my reaction the first time I picked up a copy of *The Gospel According to Peanuts*, a book that gleaned spiritual insights from the comic strip way back in the early 1970s. My first thought was, *Wow, this is so cool! There's spiritual stuff in a comic strip!* My second thought was prophetic: *They're not gonna like this!* "They," of course, being the church. What I didn't know was that the book had been released several years earlier, and sure enough, a lot of "them" didn't like it, not one bit. How could there be a gospel according to anyone but Matthew, Mark, Luke, or John? Utter blasphemy! And then, of all the nerve, Robert Short wrote a sequel, *The Parables of Peanuts* — a further assault on the sacredness of Scripture! You could almost hear the collective fainting of the highly offended saints.

But many of us loved the books, even if we did feel the need to hide our copies under the mattress in case some professional Christians happened to drop by unexpectedly. There was stuff in those books that actually poked fun at the church. But the real genius behind the appeal of *Peanuts* to those of us who were postmoderns-in-waiting was, of course, cartoonist Charles Schulz's gift for presenting deep spiritual truth through the simplest of words and drawings. Unlike countless writers who have dumbed-down the gospel over the years, Schulz used a sophisticated and intelligent blend of subtlety, humor, and an extraordinary insight into human nature to convey a prophetic message to both society and the church. (Except whenever Woodstock talked. That was just fun.)

Read these books, and you'll never again read the *Peanuts* comic strip the way you used to. Don't misunderstand me: instead of ruining your enjoyment of the strip, Short's insights will enhance it.

The Gospel According to Peanuts, by Robert Short (Richmond, VA: Westminster/John Knox Press, 1965).

Aleksandr Solzhenitsyn 📖

The Gulag Archipelago

Aleksandr Solzhenitsyn experienced firsthand the capricious whims of a succession of Russian governments. Although he was a decorated war hero, he was arrested and sentenced to a labor camp in 1945 for criticizing Stalin's handling of the war. He was released on the day Stalin died in 1953, which should have been a good thing, but he was banished to central Russia, which was not a good thing. Nearly ten years later, Soviet Premier Nikita Khrushchev — whose legacy in the minds of most Americans consists almost entirely of a single shoe-pounding incident — read Solzhenitsyn's anti-Stalin novella, *One Day in the Life of Ivan Denisovich*, and reportedly loved it, making that the only thing I ever had in common with dear Nikita, as far as I know.

But alas, Khrushchev found himself in the doghouse and was booted out of office; the new Soviet regime decided they didn't like Solzhenitsyn and refused to publish his works. But his manuscripts found their way to the West, and in 1970 he was awarded the Nobel Prize for Literature, which again should have been a good thing, but he couldn't leave the Soviet Union to accept the award. Finally, the Soviets must have figured he was far more trouble than he was worth, and in 1974 they banished him forever. Or at least, as it turned out, until the Soviets were banished forever.

Several years after his exile, Solzhenitsyn emigrated to the United States, where he proceeded to alternately enchant and offend the media and the masses. At first he was a media darling and a trophy émigré for the American government: "Look! A Russian who found faith in a prison camp and got out and chose to live *where?* In the U.S., of course!" But he fell out of favor when he began criticizing the West for its complacency, lack of moral courage, and legalistic attitudes.

I ignored the backlash and concentrated on what Solzhenitsyn had to say, mainly through *Ivan Denisovich* and his monumental multivolume work, *The Gulag Archipelago*, a disturbing account of life in the Soviet labor camp system that was based on his observations as a prisoner as well as the experiences of other prisoners. The Soviets did not take kindly to this exposé, which is why they finally booted him out. The combination of the depth of his faith and the courage it took for him to stand up for his convictions stood in marked contrast to what I saw in the church at that time (and, well, what I saw in my own life). I thought we could use a few more troublemakers like him. I still do.

The Gulag Archipelago, by Aleksandr Solzhenitsyn (New York: HarperCollins, 1974–1978).

Sheldon Vanauken 📖

A Severe Mercy

Of all the books I've read in my adult years, I can recall only one that actually moved me to tears. Sheldon Vanauken's *A Severe Mercy,* a deeply moving, deeply personal account of a love relationship that ended in tragedy, was that book. Not only did it make me cry, it made me cry twice. I lent my copy to some sneaky book thief but reread it when I received a publisher's copy of an edition known as Davy's Edition, which included photos not contained in the original release. In truth, the book made me cry three times, because I broke down in tears as I looked at the photos even before I read the book a second time. And then I lost *that* copy.

At the heart of the relationship between Sheldon Vanauken and Jean Davis, nicknamed Davy, was a series of pacts they made early on. Convinced that theirs was a love that is rarely seen in real life, they in a sense created their own world, complete with a "Shining Barrier" that would forever protect their love. Their devotion to each other was so intense that following their secret marriage they made a conscious decision not to have children, which was not a typical choice for a couple in the 1940s.

Then came trouble — in the form of C. S. Lewis, whom they met at Oxford. Christianity had started encroaching on their well-manicured turf, and at first they were able to laugh it off even as they found themselves increasingly puzzled by the brilliant minds that embraced such an outdated and irrelevant faith. Not surprisingly, Lewis eventually convinced them of the validity of Christ's claims.

That drove the first wedge in their relationship, as Sheldon came to realize that Davy loved God more than she loved him. They survived that, but Davy would not survive a rare liver disorder that took her life when she was only in her late twenties, as I recall.

That in itself makes for a remarkable book, made even better by Vanauken's craftsmanship as a writer. But woven into the text are eighteen letters to Sheldon from Lewis, including one sent after Davy's death, the letter from which the book's title was taken: "You have been treated with a severe mercy. You have been brought to see...that you were jealous of God. So from 'us' you have been led back to 'us and God'; it remains to go on to 'God and us.' She was further in than you, and she can help you more where she now is than she could have done on earth," Lewis wrote, in part in an effort to discourage Vanauken from committing suicide. Lewis's letters are a bonus that reveals his fondness for the couple and the compassion he showed when he had to deliver a tough message to a grieving friend.

If I can make it through the end of the current year without reading this book again, I'll be surprised. I'm overdue for a good, long cry, and I know *A Severe Mercy* will do the trick.

A Severe Mercy, by Sheldon Vanauken (San Francisco: HarperSanFrancisco, 1977).

Four

DANGEROUS JOURNEY

The Spiritually Subversive Role of Children's Literature

So now I'm married and pregnant and thinking about school again. Isn't that what good parents think about before their first child is born? Things like which is the best school district and which elementary school has the fewest problems and which one has the best teacher-to-student ratio and which neighborhood is in which school district. Well, we figured all that out in the first trimester. The best school district, the one with the fewest problems and best teacher-to-student ratio, was right in our home, and we already lived in the neighborhood.

We knew then, as postmoderns know today, that our witness is only as effective as our lives are. Teaching our children was only part of the equation; we also had to model lives of authentic faith. *Telling* a person about God is far less important than *showing* who God is by the way we live. Our children — and the surrounding culture —

want to see if our faith works in the real world. We need to show the evidence of an authentic, transformed life. We may not know in this lifetime how successful we've been at that.

The jury is also still out on how John and I fared as teachers. But because our daughters had the combined experience of home school, private school, and public school, if they really mess up there's only a one in three chance it's our fault.

Two things I know for sure: We exposed them to some marvelous books from a variety of traditions, and we didn't kill any early passion they had for reading.

Oliver Hunkin 📖

Dangerous Journey

Along about the mid-1980s I discovered one of the greatest benefits to having children. So wonderful is this benefit that I recommend going out and rounding up stray children if you can't find any in your own home. The benefit is this: you get to read all manner of books that you wouldn't be caught dead reading without a child around. One example is *Dangerous Journey*, the single best condensation of John Bunyan's *The Pilgrim's Progress* on the market. Written for children in roughly the nine- to twelve-year-old "middle reader" category, the book features extensive selections from Bunyan's original text, which editor Oliver Hunkin selected for this edition, and masterful artwork by Alan Parry.

Call it blasphemy, call it cheating, call it what you like, but back when my children were little and my reading list was extensive, I loved having this book at my fingertips. I used every excuse I could find to read *Dangerous Journey* aloud to my daughters because I got as much out of it as they did, if not more. Who had time to reread *The Pilgrim's Progress* with two young children to train and nurture and teach? Here was a condensed version, not watered down, not dumbed down through a contemporary rewriting, that I could read with complete abandon — in fact, the more often, the better! At the pediatrician's office, at nap time (theirs, not mine), at bedtime, I was the perfectly attentive mother, reading to my children at every possible opportunity. Never mind that the illustrations scared the daylights out of them, which was not surprising since my daughters were significantly younger than the recommended age group.

There are worse things in life than getting caught reading a children's book. Rather than miss out on Bunyan's classic altogether — which I think many people do, because the original seems so archaic — round up some children if you must, or just take a risk and read it on your own. Don't ignore Bunyan when Hunkin's edition is so accessible and enjoyable.

Dangerous Journey, ed. Oliver Hunkin, illustrations by Alan Parry (Grand Rapids, MI: Eerdmans, 1985).

Laura Ingalls Wilder 📖

The Long Winter

I was well into my thirties before I knew anything about Laura Ingalls Wilder apart from a mention in the credits for the TV program *Little House on the Prairie*. For all I knew, she was some obscure writer who penned a sweet little series of stories that Michael Landon happened to like. And then I discovered her books. Maybe it's because I love the way my husband reads aloud, maybe it's because we lived in a little house in the woods at the time, or maybe it's because I was just ready for it. For whatever reason, I was completely enchanted by the series and looked forward, as my children did, to my husband's nightly reading of one of the five books. Particularly riveting was *The Long Winter,* which for years I read privately during the dark days of December, even long after we had moved to the sunny warmth of Florida. There was something in that book that spoke of the power and cyclical nature of, well, nature, something that an old Indian knew by instinct and tradition and warned the settlers about: every seven years the blizzards would come, one after the other, blinding and freezing and crippling everything that became lost in the unrelenting swirls of snow. People and animals alike would succumb to the danger unless they took precautions — serious precautions.

The Indian's prediction came true. That winter was the seventh year since the last round of blizzards, and

Wilder's retelling of the extreme difficulties the settlers faced is to me a masterpiece of pioneer writing. (And yes, I know, some people suspect that Rose Wilder, Laura's daughter, actually wrote the books, but frankly, that makes little difference to me.) Like the rest of the series, this volume was written for children but makes for a satisfying read for adults as well. On a surface level, *The Long Winter* may do nothing more than remind you how utterly easy life is these days, even for many of the less fortunate. But on a deeper level, the book speaks to the profound resilience of human nature. It's the only book in which Pa Ingalls comes even close to losing it, but when he does, you realize how much sooner you would have lost it under the circumstances. Fear, faith, trust, determination, community, sacrifice, generosity (and its opposite) — Laura was witness to an enormous range of human emotions and behaviors that year, when she was just a young girl. Thankfully, she remembered it vividly, and recounted it for us to appreciate.

The Long Winter, by Laura Ingalls Wilder (New York: HarperCollins, 1971).

📖 Paul Brand and Philip Yancey
Fearfully & Wonderfully Made

At the point in our homeschooling journey when it was time to learn about the human body, I searched bookstore shelves for a meaningful book to supplement the science curriculum I planned to use. Remember those pre-Internet days? We were at the mercy of library resources like *Books in Print,* but more often than not, it seemed, neither the library nor the few bookstores in our rural area had any of the titles that sounded most intriguing. I probably had to get Paul Brand and Philip Yancey's book through mail order, hoping that the homeschoolers who recommended it knew what they were talking about.

I doubt that I ever used *Fearfully & Wonderfully Made* during our school time, since my children were a bit young for it at the time. But I read it from cover to cover, fascinated by Brand's experiences as a doctor, his humility in light of those experiences, and the spiritual insights he gleaned from them. He explored analogies between the various parts of the human body and the differing functions within the body of Christ in a way that makes the body sound so incredibly exciting. That's a fairly substantial challenge, but he and Yancey pulled it off.

Ever since Yancey made Brand's name known to the public, most people have associated Brand with what I believe is still the only leprosy hospital in the country, the U.S. Public Health Service Hospital in Carville, Louisiana. Few diseases make people recoil with horror the way leprosy does—that is, among those who realize the disease still exists. When Brand's association with the disease became widely known, he gained almost legendary stature among Yancey's readers. Throughout the book, he tells heartbreaking stories about his Carville patients and others who have suffered not only the physical effects of leprosy but also the social stigma attached to it. The metaphorical implications for the body of Christ could hardly be more apparent.

And to my sheer delight, Brand expressed a much broader understanding of the church than was generally expressed among evangelicals at the time. He wrote about the intellectual dishonesty and self-contradiction of Christian students he knew who embraced the theory of evolution in school but denied it in church. Until he was able to come to terms with beliefs like that for himself, he "determined that my faith was based on realities that could stand by themselves and that did not need to be subordinated to any explanation of science. Either I would discover that evolution was compatible with the God of my faith, or I would find that evolution was somehow wrong and I would stay with my faith.... In the Christian world I sometimes must live like this, making choices which contain inherent uncertainty." His honesty was a refreshing departure from the prevailing attitude of evangelical certainty.

Fearfully & Wonderfully Made, by Paul Brand and Philip Yancey (Grand Rapids, MI: Zondervan, 1987).

Ruth Nulton Moore

The Christmas Surprise

In 1755, skirmishes between opposing forces in the French and Indian War wreaked havoc on the small settlements that dotted the landscape of the American wilderness. One of those settlements was the Moravian village of Bethlehem, Pennsylvania, which faced the threat of certain Indian attack in December of that year. But the attack never occurred.

That's the brief account you're likely to come across in secular history books, whose editors and publishers are inclined to be skittish about matters of faith. But there's more to this story than the bare bones historical account, and we have Ruth Nulton Moore and Herald Press to thank for keeping the full story alive in *The Christmas Surprise.*

In this fictionalized account, a young girl named Kate harbors bitterness and hatred toward the Indians for burning down her house, killing her parents, and capturing her younger brother. Knowing that another Indian attack is imminent, she cannot understand the thinking of Bethlehem's devout townspeople, who make the decision to stay within the town's stockade rather than try to escape the slaughter to come. Christmas is just days away. The adults have been planning a surprise for the children for some time, and they decide to proceed with those plans. Meanwhile, the threat of an attack escalates.

On Christmas Eve — unbeknownst to the villagers — the Indians take their positions outside the stockade, awaiting the signal to begin the attack. Inside the stockade, just before daybreak three men take *their* positions, ready to awaken the people for the Christmas surprise. At first light, the village men herald the coming of the newborn King with the sleep-shattering sound of trombones — a sound foreign to the ears of the Indians. Fearing for their lives at this strange and frightening noise, the Indians turn tail and flee. The townspeople are spared — all because of a celebration marking the arrival of their Lord.

What's striking about this wonderful story is the complete lack of an "us versus them" mentality. The townspeople didn't arrogantly assume God would spare them because they were his favored ones. They didn't command God to rain down death and destruction on their enemies. They just quietly and calmly went about their everyday lives and followed through with the plans they had made, always confident of God's presence but never presumptuous about his will. As a result, the conflict ended peacefully without a single life being lost.

Moore wrote a follow-up story, *A Distant Thunder*, which I never read. But now, after refreshing my memory about this marvelous children's book, I think I might have to.

The Christmas Surprise, by Ruth Nulton Moore (Scottdale, PA: Herald Press, 1989).

Ben Carson and Cecil Murphey 📖
Gifted Hands

Snow is my very favorite weather event, and yes, I do rank weather events according to my liking. In southern Delaware, a snowfall isn't exactly a given, and during most of the five winters we spent there we saw a light dusting at best. But one year, we more than made up for it, with so much snow and ice that it disrupted our lives all winter long. One of the biggest disappointments that year was a canceled personal appearance by Dr. Ben Carson. For months, one of our daughters had looked forward to the moment when she would be able to shake the hand of the surgeon who had operated for twenty-two hours in a successful attempt to separate Siamese twins joined at the back of the head.

In *Gifted Hands*, Carson's description of that exacting operation was so detailed, so precise, so fascinating that I nearly forgot how squeamish I am about all things medical. It's not the blood; it's all that other stuff inside us that makes my skin crawl. That, and the thought of all those raw nerves exposed to the air and the blade of a scalpel. Only for the sake of my children's education would I expose my own nerves to such torture.

Ben Carson is one of those unlikely heroes whom I loved to tell my children about. Many historical figures in the West were born to privilege and became leaders because of their bloodline, but there were also many who overcame adversity to achieve remarkable accomplish-ments. Carson is among the latter. An obstinate, angry child with failing grades who was reared in inner-city Detroit by a single mother with determination and a strong faith in God, Ben Carson eventually turned his life around, graduating at the top of his high school class, earning a scholarship to Yale University, and complet-ing his medical degree at the University of Michigan Medical School. He pioneered a risky surgical procedure on the brain called a hemispherectomy that gives some terminally ill children an opportunity for a longer life.

Coauthor Cecil Murphey is one of the unsung heroes of the evangelical Christian publishing industry, with something like a hundred books to his credit. But most of that credit is only privately acknowledged, since many of his books were ghostwriting projects. I like to give ink where ink is due, so this ink is Murphey's as well as Carson's.

Gifted Hands, by Ben Carson and Cecil Murphey (Grand Rapids, MI: Zondervan, 1992).

📖 Roland H. Bainton
Here I Stand: A Life of Martin Luther

If I ruled the world, history teachers would be required to teach history primarily through the use of well-written biographies along the lines of David McCullough's *John*

Adams. There'd be a back-and-forth discussion in classes, from elementary school on, about people and their ideas and actions and how they affected other people and other groups of people. In the course syllabus for sixteenth-century European history, *Here I Stand* would have a place on the required reading list.

Roland Bainton's biography of Martin Luther reveals the myriad factors that combined to prompt Luther to take his stand against the Catholic Church, an act that resulted in the Protestant Reformation. The author's detailed and thorough analysis frees both the man and the movement from the typical, one-dimensional portrayal presented in too many history textbooks. Like any good biography, this one also shows the emotional struggles that Luther endured both before and after the pivotal event he's best known for, posting the ninety-five theses that criticized certain doctrines and practices of the church. The book also provides a great opportunity for young people to learn about Luther as a man in relation to his family and to his personal faith, not just about his public proclamation of that faith.

So maybe I won't ever rule the world, but I'm hoping some history teacher somewhere will recognize the wisdom of my recommendation and get in the habit of putting a human face on history.

Here I Stand: A Life of Martin Luther, by Roland H. Bainton (Copyright by Pierce and Smith, 1950. Copyright renewed by Roland H. Bainton 1977. Hardcover edition by Abingdon Press, Nashville, 1980. Meridian paperback edition by The Penguin Group 1995).

📖 Louise Rankin
Daughter of the Mountains

This is where I should insert a plug for Sonlight Curriculum, a homeschooling resource company (online at *www.sonlight.com*). The year we used Sonlight was our last year of full-time homeschooling, and I wish I'd given it a try much sooner. Sonlight's philosophy of education is so close to my own that it's no wonder I was drawn to it; the company provides an entire year's curriculum composed of individual books — real books, not textbooks (except for skills courses like math). Every book the company provided was memorable. In fact, every entry on the list at the end of this chapter is a book we read as part of the Sonlight program.

Louise Rankin uses a wonderful device to take young readers on a trek through a part of the world that remains a mystery to most people: Tibet, Bhutan, Nepal, and India. Momo is a young girl from Tibet who more than anything wants a Lhasa apso dog, which is much more pet than her family can afford. She miraculously receives one, but one night the puppy is stolen by a traveling band of thieves. Realizing what they've done, Momo sets out in search of her beloved dog, Pempa. In each village along the main "highway," she learns of the thieves' progress as they make their way toward India, and she follows their trail with a tenacity fueled by the love she has for her pet.

The pet angle is enough to keep a child absorbed in the story. But along the way, as young readers anxiously keep reading to find out how the story will turn out, they can't help but learn about the different cultures and different religions Momo encounters in her travels. The land itself, from the soaring and treacherous Himalayas to the dusty streets of Calcutta, comes alive in Rankin's story. *Daughter of the Mountains* is of course an inspiring story — have you ever known a children's book that wasn't? — but it also provides children (and their parents) with a glimpse into the beliefs and traditions of various ethnic groups.

Daughter of the Mountains, by Louise Rankin (New York: Puffin Books, 1989).

Also Recommended

Quang Nhuong Huynh / *The Land I Lost*

Fifteen stories tell about the author's childhood in Vietnam, in which encounters with wild and dangerous animals — including the deadly horse snake and a "pet" water buffalo named Tank — play a prominent role. I wish the author had done more than simply touch on

the war, but still, the book offers a look at a way of life
that has since disappeared.

(New York: HarperCollins, 1986).

John and Helen Dekker / *Torches of Joy:*
A Stone Age Tribe's Encounter with the Gospel

One of the mainstays of the Sonlight Curriculum is
missionary literature. This outstanding book traces the
experiences of a missionary family who ministered to the
Dani people of New Guinea, who as late as the 1960s had
no idea what metal was. As far as I know, all Sonlight-
recommended books on missions focus on those stories
in which the Christians respected the native culture and
avoided the temptation to impose Western culture on the
people.

(Seattle: YWAM Publishing, 1996).

Susan Fletcher / *Shadow Spinner*

This one will stay with you for a while — a long while.
It's a retelling of the Scheherazade legend in which a
young girl helps Scheherazade by tracking down the
source of a particular story that the sultan likes, as well as
some new ones. Every character in Susan Fletcher's book
is memorable. In fact, pretty much everything about the
book is memorable. We all loved this one.

(Dallas: Aladdin, 1999).

Barbara Cohen / *Seven Daughters and Seven Sons*

Another memorable book, this one is the story of the daughter of a poor merchant who defies her culture's attitude toward women and refuses to accept the traditional role of women in her Arab society. The story is based on an ancient Iraqi folk story in which a young girl disguises herself as a boy, joins a caravan, and sets off for a faraway port where she becomes a highly successful businessman — I mean, businesswoman. The feminist angle never feels forced or contrived.

(New York: HarperCollins, 1994).

Five

SOLA SCRIPTURA

Legalism, Charismania, and Truth

The biblical book of Exodus describes a time when God provided food for the wandering Israelites in the form of manna, believed to be a bread-like substance. There was a hitch to God's provision, though. The manna quickly rotted (or melted, depending on the Bible translation), and the Israelites were warned against trying to horde any for future use.

The manna principle, it seems, applies to books as well. In the early 1990s, my friend Rita invited me to look through several boxes of Christian books she planned to give away, so I could see whether there were any titles that I wanted. I was familiar with nearly every one of her books, or at least every author represented in the three cartons. I couldn't find a single one I wanted. "I know," Rita said, indicating that we were on the same wavelength. "It's like rotten manna, isn't it?"

It was fitting that those particular books had gone bad on us. They were all written by authors who were

120

leaders in the charismatic movement, which was characterized in part by an emphasis on what was called God's "now" word. The idea was that just as the prophets of old spoke specific words of warning and wisdom to their cultures, today's "prophets" spoke not only to individual societies but also to individual congregations. A "prophet" — sorry, but I can't avoid the overuse of quotation marks here — may have had a specific word from God that applied only to the people assembled in a particular building at a particular time.

I guess that's why so few books from that era have held up well. The emphasis on God's "now" word turned out to be a self-fulfilling prophecy; what the authors wrote when "now" meant the 1970s and 1980s no longer applied by the 1990s and later. I don't mean to imply that there were no good books written by charismatic authors during that time, but it does seem that very few had a significant shelf life.

In order to be a mission to the culture around us, we need to relate to the culture in relevant and intelligible ways. That means dropping the Christian jargon (do I hear another "Amen!"? Or is that jargon? Oh, the challenges!) in favor of the words and symbols and ideas and pictures that secular postmoderns use to communicate with each other. Theirs is a media-rich vocabulary, with their very thought patterns formed and informed by constantly changing multimedia experience and technology. Their frame of reference is decidedly post-Christian;

we cannot assume they have a clue as to what we're talking about, which is why we should talk a whole lot less than we have been. Today, we need to listen more and communicate better in nonverbal ways.

When I became disenchanted with the charismatic movement in the 1990s, mainly because legalism and heavy-handed control began to dominate church life, I developed a serious distrust in the writings of many of the movement's leaders. There were exceptions — Catholic and Episcopalian charismatics, for instance, whose appreciation for two thousand years of church history and tradition kept them grounded, while their deep understanding of the power of symbols kept them relevant to a postmodern culture. There were also those leaders I knew personally whose integrity was unquestioned. After a while, though, my reading narrowed down to the Bible, a few older books that shed light on parts of the Bible, and a bookcase full of reference texts. And Jamie Buckingham. Always Jamie Buckingham.

Jamie Buckingham

The Truth Will Set You Free, but First It Will Make You Miserable

About the best thing to come out of the charismatic renewal, in the printed word at least, were the columns Jamie Buckingham wrote for *Charisma* magazine and elsewhere, and the forty-some books he authored. He was our Dave Barry before even Dave Barry was Dave Barry. No one could poke fun at the church the way Jamie could and get away with it.

Buckingham told of a time when a celebrated evangelist announced that everyone in the room at a large convention would be "slain in the Spirit," which means they would fall backward onto the floor under the power of the Holy Spirit, who was apparently operating that night at the behest of the evangelist. And everyone did fall — everyone but Jamie. "My wife accused me (from her prone position under the chairs) of being stubborn, independent and rebellious. I wasn't proud of my obstinacy. In fact, I was embarrassed. But since I had to live with myself, I chose not to play games" (p. 84).

That may seem like a not-so-big deal, but if you've ever been in a situation like that, you have to appreciate how difficult it must have been for him. He was a highly visible, well-recognized leader in the charismatic movement, and the temptation to "fall" must have been great. To not fall would be seen as undermining the evangelist's words and ministry, as well as repudiating the power of the Holy Spirit. But Buckingham did not sense the power at that moment, and he refused to take a fall just to make someone else look good. In his earlier years in the pastorate, his penchant toward pride and deception had gotten in the way of his ministry, and he had made a promise to himself that he would never live an inauthentic life again. He was indeed a man after my own heart; I had enormous respect for him.

Along with *The Truth Will Set You Free, but First It Will Make You Miserable,* Buckingham also wrote "serious" books, always managing to insert some of his trademark wit. The only ones I still have are *Parables: Poking Holes in Religious Balloons* and *Power for Living.* Buckingham possessed a rare quality among charismatic writers: his work seems to have withstood the test of time. I still enjoy going back and reading bits and pieces of his books on occasion.

The Truth Will Set You Free, but First It Will Make You Miserable: The Collected Wit and Wisdom of Jamie Buckingham, by Jamie Buckingham (Altamonte Springs, FL: Creation House, 1988).

📖 Johnston M. Cheney
The Life of Christ in Stereo

Poor Johnston Cheney. The man spent twenty years working on *The Life of Christ in Stereo,* a rearranging of the Gospel accounts into a single chronological narrative. Thankfully, he did not live to see the advent of the personal computer, which would have shaved some nineteen-plus years off his efforts. That Cheney ever started the project is remarkable in itself. As he told it, a serious bout with pulmonary and bronchial tuberculosis confined him to bed, so for fun and amusement (my words), he decided to make a "scrapbook of the Scriptures." What his original intention was, or what that would have ultimately looked like, I have no idea. But along the way, he got sidetracked by the Gospels. "It was in the course of this operation that I discovered by pure accident, humanly speaking, that the three accounts of Jesus' baptism, for example, could be made into one account for my scrapbook purposes and without losing anything," he wrote. From that experience, he realized that many of the problems scholars had in reconciling the Gospel narratives could be solved by creating a single, chronological text.

Well now. Determined as I was to prove to everyone with at least one ear that the Bible was indeed the word of God, I found this book to be a dream come true. At last! A book that proved the Gospels were written by a single Author: the Holy Spirit!

I was on my way toward becoming the most annoying Bible-thumper in all of central New Jersey. But I stopped long enough to read this book, and while I am fairly certain I did use it as a weapon a time or two, I discovered something far more important than ammunition for my next argument: I discovered a truly multidimensional Jesus. Reading the Gospels as a single book made me forget about the different human authors and the different audiences they were writing to. At times, Cheney's rearrangement took my breath away. It was as if I was reading about the life of Christ for the first time. I could almost imagine how a heathen on the mission field would respond to this good news. Believe me, I would believe.

The Life of Christ in Stereo, by Johnston M. Cheney (Portland, OR: Western Baptist Seminary Press, 1969).

📖 Eugene Peterson
A Long Obedience in the Same Direction

The subtitle for Eugene Peterson's book is *Discipleship in an Instant Society;* the copyright date is 1980. Don't you love it? We didn't know what an instant society was back in 1980! We were still writing letters, for Pete's sake, and talking on phones tethered to a wall and cooking in this big appliance called an oven. Maybe Peterson was a true prophet back then.

In his studies on discipleship and pilgrimage, Peterson "found, tucked away in the Hebrew Psalter, an old dog-eared songbook" — the Songs of Ascent, Psalms 120–134. He suggests that those were the psalms the Hebrew pilgrims sang as they annually went "up" to Jerusalem, the highest point in Palestine, for the feasts of Passover, Pentecost, and Tabernacles. The ascent, he believed, served as a metaphor for a "life lived upward to God." He drew the title from a passage from Friedrich

Nietzsche's *Good and Evil:* " . . . there should be long obedience in the same direction; there thereby results, and has always resulted in the long run, something which has made life worth living." But that long obedience is what the world so often discourages and thwarts.

We needed this book in 1980, and we need this book again today. I suppose some of the anecdotes and illustrations Peterson uses in his meditative commentary on each psalm could use some updating, but the central message of focused perseverance has never been more relevant.

There's a scene in an episode of *Buffy the Vampire Slayer* ("Villains," episode 20, season six, don't ask how I know) in which Willow, by this time a powerful witch, uses her powers to upload the text of an ancient book into her brain. She stands over the book and extends her arms downward, and we can see the text travel up her arms. Witchcraft and sorcery aside, I'd sure like to have that kind of power. I'd go back to all the wonderful books that meant so much to me over the years and upload them. The only alternative is to quit my life and reread every single one.

Peterson has written, oh, a few important books since *A Long Obedience in the Same Direction* — namely, the sixty-six books of the Bible in the superb paraphrase *The Message*. It's worth it to look beyond that magnum opus and seek out some of his other titles.

A Long Obedience in the Same Direction: Discipleship in an Instant Society, by Eugene Peterson (Downers Grove, IL: InterVarsity: 1980).

📖 Phillip Keller

A Shepherd Looks at Psalm 23

Even the biblically illiterate generally have a passing knowledge of Psalm 23, the one that starts, "The Lord is my shepherd," and the one that is among the most comforting passages in all of Scripture. But really, few people in the industrialized world really get the shepherd-sheep metaphor on anything but a superficial, feel-good level. So when Phillip Keller, a real-life sheep rancher, wrote *A Shepherd Looks at Psalm 23* in 1970, it became a best seller almost immediately, thanks to the author's detailed knowledge of a shepherd's role and the sheep's quirky behavior, and to his insights into the significance of the image of the Lord as the shepherd of his people.

Each chapter is devoted to a verse or line in the psalm and offers much more than a simple reflection on the passage's spiritual meaning. With Keller as an experienced guide, we are able to make sense of certain lines in the psalm that we seldom question. Our familiarity with some parts of Scripture, it seems, tends to quench our curiosity and distract us from going deeper into its meaning.

A case in point is this line from verse 2: "He makes me lie down in green pastures." Now really, why would a shepherd ever have to "make" sheep lie down? Well, Keller has the answer: sheep won't lie down unless they feel safe, sense no tension among others in the flock, are not disturbed by fleas or other pests, and are not experiencing hunger. Sheesh! How fussy can they get? Come to think of it, though, I wouldn't be able to rest very well under those circumstances. When the shepherd takes care of those problems, the flock is able to settle down and be at rest.

Shortly after I read this in 1974, the newspaper I worked for assigned me to accompany an elementary school class on a field trip to an agricultural research center affiliated with Rutgers University. While most of the class ran off to a more fascinating section of the facilities, I stayed back and spent nearly a half-hour observing the behavior of a flock of sheep. "Observing," as I reflect on the activity now, is much too scientific a term. "Meditating on" fits much better. He was absolutely right, I kept thinking. Keller was absolutely right. Granted, thirty minutes was hardly enough time to draw any hard-and-fast conclusions of my own, but it did allow me to confirm with my own eyes that the behavior of sheep is exactly as Keller described it.

And my personal experience with God has proven the Lord to be every bit the kind of shepherd Keller described. "It is no accident that God has chosen to call us sheep.... Our mass mind (or mob instinct), our fears and timidity, our stubbornness and stupidity, our perverse habits are all parallels of profound importance," he wrote on page 21. Keller changed my perception of God, even as he changed my perception of myself, his words chipping away at my human pride and arrogance.

A Shepherd Looks at Psalm 23, by Phillip Keller (Grand Rapids, MI: Zondervan, 1970).

📖 Judson Cornwall

Praying the Scriptures

Praying the Scriptures as a spiritual activity is so widely practiced in some segments of the church that it's embarrassing to admit that I never heard of it until sometime in the 1990s. Early on in my relationship with God, before I learned that spontaneous prayers were the only ones God would listen to, I used to pray portions of the Bible back to God, especially when I worked on the morning desk at a daily newspaper and had get up at 2 a.m. My brain wouldn't be fully awake for another hour or two, so praying the Psalms seemed like a pretty good way to greet God on those days. I dropped the habit when my schedule changed.

Imagine my surprise when I came across Judson Cornwall's book *Praying the Scriptures*. This guy was a leader in the charismatic movement, the same movement that taught me that reading a prayer was tantamount to cheating. Unless prayer came from your heart and was expressed in your words, it was worthless. Along came Cornwall, whose name sounded so nineteenth-century British but who in fact was twentieth-century American, suggesting that the Bible is actually a prayer book and that when we're at a loss for words we can open the pages of Scripture and pray back to God the very words God had authored. And here I thought that when we were at a loss for words, our only recourse was to pray in tongues. In the context of the charismatic world, Cornwall's words would have sounded like heresy had he not been a leader in the charismatic world. Some things are like that, I guess.

Oh, the unlearning so many of us have had to go through! It's harder than the learning because our learning was a matter of simple trust. We trusted a particular pastor or Bible teacher, so we felt confident in learning from them. For many of us, that trust has been shattered, and now, in the unlearning phase, we question everything — even the process of unlearning.

My copy of Cornwall's book, by the way, contains a rather unfortunate typo. The chapter titles all begin with "Praying the Scriptures..." and continue with a word beginning with "I" — such as, "Illuminates Our Prayer" and gives "Imagery to Our Prayer." In the table of contents, chapter 20 assures us that "Praying the Scriptures Gives Immorality to Our Prayer." Of course, it was supposed to read "Immortality." I was the unwitting bearer

of bad news to the book's editor, who was unaware of
the error until I happened to run into her and pulled a
nudge-nudge, wink-wink on her. Who knew she was in
the dark? I thought it was funny. She didn't.

*Praying the Scriptures: Communicating with God in His Own
Words*, by Judson Cornwall (Lake Mary, FL: Creation House,
1998).

Six

THE CLOISTER WALK

Discovering Liturgy and Female Writers

Soon after I became a Christian, I developed a yearning to become a nun — or something nun-like since I wasn't Catholic and had no intention of becoming Catholic. What I really wanted was the experience of living in community with other Christians, even though I knew how hard it was to live with other people. The chances that I would ever become a nun, or nunnish, were nil given all the things I'd have to sacrifice, none of which I could live without.

Another drawback was that nuns used a book called a missal, and that creeped me out. The name sounded weird enough — do we really need a book, I wondered, that sounds like an airborne weapon? — but even worse, the contents followed a strict liturgical format. Any real Christian knew that if Jesus wanted us to use a missal, he would have written one himself. So there was another strike against the monastic life.

Over the next twenty-five years, the lure of the monastery never completely disappeared. Ironically, that lure
is decidedly postmodern. Instead of seeing the church as
a vehicle for sending out missionaries, we postmodern
Christians consider ourselves to be a mission to the
culture around us. It's in this relationship to the surrounding culture that the postmodern church is like a
medieval monastery. That may sound like a paradox and a
step or even ten backwards. But the medieval monastery
served many vital functions, providing refuge, hospitality, and spiritual direction to those who entered its doors,
as well as performing essential and often life-saving services to the surrounding community. And while no one
that I know of is calling for an across-the-board return to
cloistered living, some Christians are following a call to
create a physical community. Most of us will continue to
live apart from each other, but as co-followers of Christ
we can still provide spiritual shelter and protection for
each other.

Anyway, I gradually became accustomed to hearing, if
not actually saying, the word "liturgy." It wasn't until I
finally reached the end of my church rope that I was able
to attend a — gasp! — liturgical service. I had exhausted
all other ecclesiastical possibilities; only the Episcopal
Church, with its endless rites and rituals, remained. To
my utter astonishment, I loved it.

One thing I learned right away about many Episcopalians: they sure love to read. They'll read anything and

everything, especially books banned by libraries. These were my kind of people. And the writers! Some of the most highly respected, widely read authors of theological books were — gender gasp! — *women.* It was time to head to the bookstore yet again.

Kathleen Norris 📖

The Cloister Walk

No other writer has fed my yearning for the monastic life the way Kathleen Norris has. Since I first came into contact with monks and nuns when I became religion editor for a New Jersey newspaper in the 1970s, I've longed for the life they live, though I imagine I romanticized it far too much at first. As I began to spend more time with nuns in particular, I began to sense the tremendous difficulty of living in a convent. Apart from the obvious renunciation of what we consider normal living, they also had to put up with each other day in and day out. At times, the tension was palpable, even to me, an outsider and only occasional visitor.

What I did not learn until I read *The Cloister Walk* was that the monastic experience was available to the likes of me. Though I enjoyed two of Norris's other books (*Dakota* and *Amazing Grace: A Vocabulary of Faith*) much more, I have to admit that this one had a greater impact on me. I immediately began to explore the possibility of staying at a monastery. It took a while for me to follow through, since none of my friends were quite as monastically inclined as I was at the time, and going it alone was a bit daunting. But I did it, and I have Norris to thank for opening up the doors of the monastery for me and beckoning me to enter.

Not only did she cure me of cloisterphobia, she also introduced me to a host of female writers on spirituality. Steeped as I was in the evangelical and charismatic traditions at the time, I knew of precious few female Christian writers who were highly regarded in their own right. Most female charismatic writers (but not all) had acquired a platform only through their husbands' ministries. The exceptions, like Kay Arthur and Marilyn Hickey and Joyce Meyer, were few and far between. Reading Norris led me to books by Anne Lamott and Sarah York and Annie Dillard and countless others. Who knew there was this world of women out there writing the kinds of books I wish I had written?

Dakota is one of those books, though mine would have been called *Wyoming*. Some days my longing for Wyoming is so intense that I nearly become convinced that somebody came along and stole my life from me, depositing me in Florida instead of the Rockies. Norris's book-length meditation on the spirituality of the land and the people in the Dakota Plains, oddly enough, only makes the longing more real to me. The Rockies are hardly the Plains, but still. There's that vastness that the two areas have in common, a vastness where I always, always, experience the vastness of God.

The Cloister Walk, by Kathleen Norris (New York: The Penguin Group, Riverhead hardcover 1996, paperback 1997).

Anne Lamott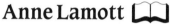

Traveling Mercies

Anne Tyler, Annie Dillard, Annie Proulx, Anne Rice, Ann Rule, Anne Lamott — at one point a few years ago I seriously considered writing under my mother's name, Ann Edwards, because just about every author I was reading at the time was named some variation of Ann. Plus, they were all so bloody successful. Maybe there really was something about seeing that name on a book cover that prompted people to buy all those books. It was worth a shot, I figured, but then I factored in the talent quotient. I didn't want to go down in publishing history as the only failed author named Ann or Annie or Anne.

Anne Lamott comes by her Anne-the-writer success honestly. She's witty to the point of irreverence, which not surprisingly endears her to me no matter what she writes about. "My friends like to tell each other that I am not really a born-again Christian. They think of me more along the lines of that old Jonathan Miller routine, where he said, 'I'm not really a Jew — I'm Jew-ish.' They think I am Christian-ish," she wrote. "But I'm not. I'm just a bad Christian. A bad born-again Christian."

Before her born-againness took root, Lamott battled addiction to alcohol and drugs and had an affair with a married man that ended with her becoming pregnant and subsequently having an abortion. The abortion was not without complications, and one night during her recovery she sensed the presence of someone in her room. She had no doubt it was Jesus. What she wrote next is probably one of the most widely quoted sections of *Traveling Mercies,* but it's so good that I can't help myself: "I thought about my life and my brilliant hilarious progressive friends, I thought about what everyone would think of me if I became a Christian. And . . . I turned to the wall and said out loud, 'I would rather die.' " Jesus, whom she never actually sees with her eyes, stays with her through the night. She thought she could shake off the experience, but no. "Everywhere I went, I had the feeling that a little cat was following me . . . wanting me to open the door and let it in. But I knew what would happen: you let a cat in one time, give it a little milk, and then it stays forever."

Like C. S. Lewis, Anne Lamott was indeed one reluctant convert.

Lamott's *Bird by Bird* is one of the few books on writing that I consistently recommend to my writing workshop students. The story from which the book derives its title, which Lamott tells in the chapter "Short Assignments," contains a priceless nugget of wisdom for any writer overwhelmed by a daunting writing assignment.

Traveling Mercies, by Anne Lamott (New York: Doubleday/ Anchor Books, 2000).

Paula D'Arcy 📖

Gift of the Red Bird

By the time *Gift of the Red Bird* was published, readers were already aware of Paula D'Arcy's tragic loss of her husband and baby daughter some twenty years earlier. But D'Arcy's healing from her inexpressible pain and sorrow was far in the future when *Song for Sarah,* based on her journal entries as she processed her grief, was released in 1979, four years after the car crash that killed her family.

With *Gift of the Red Bird,* D'Arcy takes us inside her healing process. It's an intensely personal account of a journey into the wilderness and an encounter with God that quite literally restored her soul. "There is one advantage to having your life cut through to the bone. It swiftly eliminates all the distractions and all the illusions.... If I am going to encounter God, he will find no resistance. ... I am split open. God will come all the way in, if he is out there at all," she wrote in 1975 (p. 32).

Fourteen years later, toward the end of a three-day vision quest, her senses came alive as they never had before. "The flies and the bee, the river and the red bird...all of them have worked so hard to open my heart and expand my sight. I never lived inside my own wilderness before, and they are the only companions to that world that I have....How will I explain to my human world that these creatures have unerringly and purposefully been my teachers?"

There's a particular type of poignancy to all of D'Arcy's books, one that never feels forced as it might at the hands of a lesser writer. In two subsequent books, the anecdotal *A New Set of Eyes* and the Scripture-based devotional *Searching with All My Heart,* she gives us another look into her ever-seeking spirit and at the truths she gleans from everyday life.

One of the reasons her way of expressing her faith resonates with me is that in some respects her spiritual journey resembles mine. During the 1980s, she had studied other faiths and realized that God was much larger than the one she had been taught about. "In many places where my religious programming insisted issues were black and white, I kept finding a great Mystery....I began to ask myself how we could learn all the things God wanted to teach us if we limited our intake with fear. I saw fear everywhere: the common fear of having to think in a new way; fear of listening to other spiritual points of view; fear of new revelations about God that didn't fit comfortably with existing ideas and opinions."

I used to hear people outside evangelicalism talk about the fear that drove evangelicals, and I'd wonder what on earth they were talking about. Now I know. Now I see the fear that did drive us and continues to drive so many in the evangelical fold. Whatever it was that lit a fire under the Brian McLarens and the Leonard Sweets (see chapter 7) and all the other evangelicals who started listening and questioning and going public with it all, whatever it was — thank God for it.

Gift of the Red Bird, by Paula D'Arcy (New York: Crossroad, 1996).

Thomas Keating 📖

Intimacy with God

No one does a better job of explaining the practice of centering prayer than Thomas Keating does, and that includes me. He describes it as a means of preparing for the act of contemplation, a way of reducing the noise in our minds so we can open our spirits completely to God. Even that is a feeble paraphrase of Keating's definition, and as he points out in *Intimacy with God,* the definition of the word "contemplation" has become so ambiguous that few understand its meaning. That ambiguity prompted Keating, a Trappist monk, to meet with other Catholic religious as well as monks from other faith traditions to develop a way to teach centering prayer to retreatants and to bring out the gift of contemplation in others.

I don't claim to be a contemplative, especially after Keating convinced me that few of us even know what that means. All I'll say is, I've been drawn to the contemplative tradition all of my adult life, whether I acted on it or not. Most of the time I was distracted by whatever tradition I was hooked up with at the time. I will also say this: My experience with centering prayer has brought me into a greater level of intimacy with God than I've ever known before, which certainly underscores the accuracy of Keating's book's title.

Throughout the book, Keating refers to *The Cloud of Unknowing,* a fourteenth-century text by an unknown writer. Before I read Keating, I read *The Cloud of Unknowing* — but only after I was able to get past the chilling warning at the beginning that basically tells all but the most serious readers to back off and fast. The fact that it's addressed to "Christian men" and "ghostly friend" also gave me pause, given the warning and all. The writer continued: "Fleshly janglers, open praisers and blamers of themselves or of any other, tellers of trifles, runners and tattlers, and all manner of pinchers, cared I never that they saw this book." I really didn't know whether to keep reading beyond that sentence since I didn't know what a couple of those words meant, but then I remembered that I'd be violating the gender exclusion no matter what. So I kept reading. As far as I could, anyway. My mind started wandering big time along about chapter 4 — with fifty-four chapters to go. I wondered, Is it possible that there's a Cliff Notes version for *The Cloud of Unknowing?* When I discovered Keating, I figured he could be my personal Cliff Notes edition and tell me all I really needed to know about that book.

An earlier book by Keating, *Open Mind, Open Heart: The Contemplative Dimension of the Gospel,* also explains centering prayer, but it is based on a different series of seminars he gave. Both books include thorough and helpful appendices. I have a nagging feeling that I once read *Awakenings*, Keating's book on the ministry of Jesus, but I couldn't testify to it in a court of law. Probably worth reading, though.

Intimacy with God: An Introduction to Centering Prayer, by Thomas Keating (New York: Crossroad, 1994).

Robert Ellsberg 📖

All Saints

All Saints occupies a place of honor and distinction in our home. It lies atop a sofa table where it's both visible and accessible. Everyone who lives here knows not to mess with it, including Sonny the cat who took to chewing book covers after his beloved mate, Cher, moved on to a better life. All our other books share shelf space with several thousand titles, or are piled on the floor until more bookcases arrive, or are thrown into a half-dozen or so baskets earmarked for the writing, editing, and teaching projects I'm working on at any given time. *All Saints* requires nothing less than its own sacred space. Heaven help the person who carelessly drops a set of keys — or worse, places a coffee mug — on top of it.

I read Robert Ellsberg's book every day. Or at least I intend to. It helps that it's arranged in a daily format, with each day of the year given over to a brief reflection on either a church-endorsed saint or some unendorsed person whose life or work provides an unforgettable picture of God's love and grace. Among the former, there are the expected: Augustine, Aquinas, Teresa of Avila. Among the latter, there are the unexpected: Albert Camus, Vincent van Gogh, Dag Hammerskjöld (whose *Markings* very nearly warranted its own entry in *this* book). I love the mix of people Robert Ellsberg chose to include, and I never tire of rereading each day's entry, year after year. When I realize I've missed a day or two or three, I go back and catch up — not because I'm obsessive-compulsive, though I'm not denying that, but because I cannot abide the thought of what I might have missed.

Imagine zoning out on May 11 and missing the wonderful story of sixteenth-century Jesuit missionary Matteo Ricci, who won over the skeptical Chinese people he served and found common ground between

Confucian ethics and Christian morality. Or sleeping in on February 12 and overlooking the entry for C. F. Andrews, who taught in India in the early twentieth century and became such an exemplary model of witnessing to the gospel through deeds that Mohandas Gandhi suggested all missionaries copy his methods. Or using the busyness of the season as an excuse to avoid reading the entry for December 20 — the always stirring account of the life of Raoul Wallenberg, the Hungarian Jews' "last and only hope" of protection from the Nazis. Miss out on any of that? May it never be!

With nearly every reading, I am at the same time pumped by the realization of what one person in service to God can accomplish and distressed at my own inadequate service to God.

But here's the weird and beautiful thing: I always close the book with the pumped side winning out.

All Saints: Daily Reflections on Saints, Prophets, and Witnesses for Our Time, by Robert Ellsberg (New York: Crossroad, 1997).

Henri Nouwen 📖

Life of the Beloved

Prompted by the suggestion of a Jewish man with whom he enjoyed a longstanding friendship, Henri Nouwen began setting down his thoughts on the spiritual life in the form of a series of letters to a secular friend.

The result was this intensely personal little book, not
Nouwen's best-known but one that brought me back
to an awareness of my standing as one whom God has
chosen. (Nouwen uses the word "chosen" carefully, urg-
ing his readers to cling to it regardless of the world's
misunderstanding of the term.)

Because he was writing to a friend who was immersed
in city life — New York City to be precise — Nouwen
attempted to place the "life of the Beloved" in the context
of living out a spiritual life in a secular environment teem-
ing with noise and commotion. With his Jewish friend,
that attempt failed, his friend gently explaining that truly
secular people have a whole lot of hurdles to get past
before they can even begin to assimilate the concept of
"chosenness." But the letters resonated with Nouwen's
Christian friends, who read the letters to help him deter-
mine whether he should have the manuscript published.
To our great benefit, they convinced him that his effort to
explain to a secular world how God sees us would prove
to be of immense value to the Christian world.

If you're curious as to how I chose the books to
include in *God Between the Covers,* one quote from Nouwen's book comes very close to summing up my ration-
ale. "The limited, sometimes broken, love of those who
share our humanity can often point us to the truth of who
we are: precious in God's eyes," Nouwen wrote. "This
truth is not simply an inner truth that emerges from our
center. It is also a truth that is revealed to us by the One

who has chosen us. That is why we have to keep listening to the many men and women in history who, through their lives and their words, call us back to it."

Nouwen is clearly among those who "call us back to it," to the truth revealed to us by the One who chose us.

Life of the Beloved, by Henri Nouwen (New York: Crossroad, 1992).

Book of Common Prayer

One phobia I inherited from my charismatic years was the fear of ritual and written prayers. Prayers, I was told, should be spontaneous, from the heart, suited to the situation at hand, and an intimate exchange between God and me. Well, guess what? The *Book of Common Prayer* satisfies all those requirements, especially since I can spontaneously decide which one I want to read.

My concern, though, was that I could become so familiar with it that I would miss its beauty. It was the beauty of the language that first drew me to the prayer book, and given the use I've made of it in the years I've owned it, I think I can safely predict that I won't tire of it anytime soon. How could I ever get tired of this evening prayer?

O Lord, support us all the day long, until the shadows lengthen, and the evening comes, and the busy world is hushed, and the fever of life is over, and

our work is done. Then in your mercy, grant us
a safe lodging, and a holy rest, and peace at the
last. (p. 834)

Or this wonderful morning prayer intended to be uttered
by a sick person?

This is another day, O Lord. I know not what it will
bring forth, but make me ready, Lord, for whatever
it may be. If I am to stand up, help me to stand
bravely. If I am to sit still, help me to sit quietly. If
I am to lie low, help me to do it patiently. And if I
am to do nothing, let me do it gallantly. Make these
words more than words, and give me the Spirit of
Jesus. (p. 462)

A good friend of mine prays that prayer each morning, even though she's perfectly healthy. I think that's a
great idea.

The prayer book was revised in 1979, and I still meet
people who mourn the loss of the 1929 edition. My 1929
copy — which I found in a used bookstore just a few
years ago — fell apart on me, and I've never replaced it.
The newer one suits me just fine; it contains ritual, it
contains written prayers, but it also contains truth expressed in a literary style that resonates with my spirit and
calls forth echoes of an ancient spirituality. Most of all,
the *Book of Common Prayer* offers Christians a symbol of
unity, even if it's only used by the Anglican Communion.

That's a fairly sizeable communion, and I love knowing that my prayers are linked linguistically as well as spiritually with the prayers of millions of others around the world.

Somehow, I think God will forgive me for not starting my every prayer from scratch. After all, God did give us the Lord's Prayer.

The Book of Common Prayer and Administration of the Sacraments and Other Rites and Ceremonies of the Church Together with the Psalter or Psalms of David. According to the use of The Episcopal Church. Look for a Certificate notification so that you know you are using the current approved version of the BCP. It will read: "I certify that this edition of The Book of Common Prayer has been compared with a certified copy of the Standard Book, as the Canon directs, and that it conforms thereto. Charles Mortimer Guilbert, *Custodian of the Standard Book of Common Prayer.*" A date will be listed, e.g., September 1979 or February 1990.

Richard J. Foster and James Bryan Smith 📖
Devotional Classics

Richard Foster and James Smith's compilation of fifty-two devotionals, designed to take the reader through a year of spiritual reading, draws, as the title suggests, on many classic Christian writings from the fourth through the twentieth centuries. Both authors are involved with Renovaré, a movement that has found common ground,

and works toward spiritual understanding, among the
six major streams of Christianity: contemplative, holiness, charismatic, social justice, evangelical, and incarnational — exactly the way of thinking that fuels my
postmodern sensitivities. Richard Foster describes the six
streams in his book *Streams of Living Water* in the following manner: (1) the contemplative tradition is about
discovering the life filled with prayer; (2) the holiness
tradition is about discovering and living a life of virtue;
(3) the charismatic tradition is about discovering the life
that manifests the power of the Spirit in gifts of the
Spirit; (4) the social justice tradition is about discovering
compassion for others, including the poor and misfortu-
nate and downtrodden and unaccepted groups in society;
(5) the evangelical tradition is about discovering the authority of the Bible for Christian living; and (6) the
incarnational tradition is about discovering the central-
ity of the sacraments as the means of grace for living the
Christian life and for invoking the presence of Christ in
our midst. The original *Devotional Classics* was written
some years before *Streams of Living Water* and had only
five traditions compiled. But a revised edition of *Devotional Classics* was recently published, and Foster added
the sixth stream to that compilation.

Each devotional begins with an introduction written
by Foster, whose other books (*Streams of Living Water,
Celebration of Discipline, Prayer: The Heart's True Home*, and
others) have placed him at the forefront of the spiritual

renewal movement. His introductions are followed by excerpts from some of the works and authors you'll find throughout *God Between the Covers,* like Bonhoeffer and Lewis. There are lots of other authors and works you may never have heard of or have only a passing awareness of.

George A. Buttrick, a Presbyterian minister and the author of what Foster considers one of the most thorough books on prayer, was one of those authors for me. I had this vague notion that I'd heard of him before, but I suspect I got his name mixed up with Butterick, the sewing pattern company. Because he's associated with the contemplative tradition, which I've only become acquainted with in the past decade, I think the pattern connection is the more likely one.

Also included are questions for reflection and suggested spiritual exercises that complement each entry. What I liked even more was a final section called "Going Deeper," an annotated list of other books by or about the author, which gave me carte blanche to acquire even more books.

On my shelves I have several other Renovaré resource books, all of which give me this warm and fuzzy feeling just thinking about them. I think they're as good as *Devotional Classics* is.

Devotional Classics, ed. Richard J. Foster and James Bryan Smith (San Francisco: HarperSanFrancisco, 1990, rev. ed. 2005).

📖 Thomas Merton

The Seven Storey Mountain

Back in my charismatic years, the name Thomas Merton was uttered with disdain if it was uttered at all. I cannot recall why, and I cannot figure out today how that man provoked so much contempt, leading many of us to believe his books were not worth reading. Having read three of them, I'm even more baffled. Did our Protestant pastor think we would convert to Catholicism or enter a Trappist monastery, as Merton did? Beats me.

Though Merton once said he no longer knew the man who wrote *The Seven Storey Mountain,* I still consider it the best starting point among all of Merton's books — and not just because it's an early memoir of his life and his transition from thoroughly modern Merton to Frater Louis at the Abbey of Gethsemani in Kentucky. It's also a chronicle of a secular-turned-spiritual life, lived and told authentically and reflectively.

How Merton fits into a postmodern paradigm may be difficult for some people to understand. Not only did he enter a monastery, he also sought out a life of even greater solitude when he moved to a hermitage on the grounds of Gethsemani. But Merton maintained his interaction with the world in part through his writings and through direct engagement in his later years when he left the monastery more frequently and came into contact with the wider culture. Merton developed an intense interest in Eastern spirituality, among other expressions of faith, and wrote several books on Zen Buddhism. (Ah! Of course! No wonder he was taboo!)

I would also recommend *No Man Is an Island,* but the copy I own was printed on such cheap paper that the ink spread and the type is difficult to read. What's up with that? Here's a bestselling author with a proven track record, and his publisher tries to save a couple of bucks on printing costs? I can't bring myself to read more than a few pages at a time, yet it seems irresponsible for me to consider trashing that copy and buying another. Caveat emptor and all that: open the book before you buy it, and make sure it's readable.

The Seven Storey Mountain: An Autobiography of Faith, by Thomas Merton (San Diego: Harcourt Brace, 1976).

Also Recommended

Richard Rohr / *Everything Belongs: The Gift of Contemplative Prayer*

Try to read Richard Rohr's book without underlining or highlighting something on each page — just try it. Unless you're phobic about marring a book, I'll bet you can't do it. This book is a gem, a book-length reflection on the contemplative life. Highly recommended.

(New York: Crossroad, 1999, Revised edition 2003).

Rowan Williams / *The Dwelling of the Light:*
Praying with Icons of Christ

Icons used to give me bad vibes. That was before my second or third or fourth spiritual awakening. Williams's little book serves as a great introduction to praying with icons, especially for Protestants like me who were brought up to believe that anything involving icons was akin to idol worship. He chose four representative icons to explain their use in the early church and their continued use in the Eastern Orthodox Church, offering a reflective meditation on each. Very helpful for evangelicals.

(Grand Rapids, MI: Wm. B. Eerdmans, 2003).

Gernot Candolini / *Labyrinths:*
Walking toward the Center

It's hard to believe I used to think that labyrinths were creepy and that on my one and only visit to Chartres I was too self-absorbed to notice its labyrinth. Gernot Candolini takes us along on a family pilgrimage to the labyrinths of Europe and demystifies the experience of walking a mystical path.

(New York: Crossroad, rev. English ed., 2001).

M. Basil Pennington / *Lectio Divina: Renewing the Ancient Practice of Praying the Scriptures*

Lectio Divina is an excellent introduction to the ancient practice of praying the Scriptures in a way that engages a person's entire being. The book includes a chapter on "Lectio in Cyberspace," surely one of the rare instances in which those two nouns appear together.

(New York: Crossroad, 1998).

David Hazard, ed. / *I Promise You a Crown: A 40-Day Journey in the Company of Julian of Norwich*

David Hazard's compilation of brief devotionals serves as a satisfying introduction to the writings of Julian of Norwich, who had a life-refreshing vision on her deathbed and lived another forty-three years, during which she had further visions.

(Minneapolis: Bethany House, 1995).

Ronald Rolheiser / *The Shattered Lantern: Rediscovering a Felt Presence of God*

Ronald Rolheiser first exposes and then deals with the problem of unbelief among believers who live lives of "quiet agnosticism." What we need, he wrote, is to rediscover a sense of astonishment and wonder in life and allow ourselves to be once again overwhelmed by the presence of God.

(New York: Crossroad, 1994, rev. ed., 2004).

Robert Barron / *Heaven in Stone and Glass*

Despite a whirlwind tour of some of the most famous cathedrals in France when I was a teenager, I was inexcusably ignorant of the powerful symbolism in their imagery and design. Thankfully, I discovered Robert Barron's book before I took a whirlwind tour of cathedrals in England several years ago. Worth reading even if you never visit a Gothic cathedral.

(New York: Crossroad, 2000).

Seven

A NEW KIND
OF CHRISTIAN

The Emerging Church Movement
and an Emerging Hope

Though I'm now a member of the Episcopal Church, I
still consider myself to be an evangelical . . . or evangelical-
like. Or some other word that we haven't come up with
yet. The thing is this: there's a whole lot of good in evangelicalism, but the good side — the side I identify with,
naturally — doesn't get a whole lot of press. In early 2005,
Time magazine profiled the twenty-five most influential
evangelical leaders, and the ones whose approach to faith
most closely resembled mine — like Brian McLaren —
were those that most *Time* readers had never heard of
up to that point. These leaders don't represent the Religious Right, so the press doesn't regularly seek out their
opinions.

A more inclusive, broader segment of the church that
grew out of evangelicalism has come to be known as
the "emerging church" movement — a movement that

strives to remain culturally relevant while maintaining an uncompromising commitment to Christ. The leaders of the movement ("movement" is a loose term for this dynamic process) are prolific writers, both in print and on the Internet: Dan Kimball, Tony Jones, Sally Morgenthaler, Andy Crouch, Erwin McManus, Spencer Burke, and many others, including a fair number of prominent scholars.

Though we're committed to truth — whatever that is — those of us in the emerging church hold our truths to be self-deprecating. We've learned to laugh at ourselves and our foibles and poke fun at the nutty things Christians often do in their misguided attempt to change the world. We hold our most cherished assumptions and presuppositions and dogmas lightly, remembering the many irrefutable doctrines that have crumbled before our very eyes.

If you're new to postmodernism and some of this sounds like what you've been hearing for years, that may mean one of two things: you've already been exposed to the basics of this new way of thinking and being, or — more likely — you've heard a bunch of stuff like the above that sounded good but never existed in the real world.

Let me give you an example. In most of the churches I've attended over the years, I've heard the teaching that our top three priorities should be God, family, and church, in that order. (Work sometimes comes before

church and sometimes after, depending on how legalistic — um, I mean, *radical* — the church is.) Sounds good,
but try living that way.

In some churches, you'll quickly discover that church
and God are co-equal, because church has become a god
in itself. And in this context, I mean church as in *attend-
ing* church; it seems there's nothing more offensive to
God than an empty seat, even if it means your family
suffers because you are always expected to be in your
designated spot. One of these days some church is going
to take a cue from the Academy Awards and hire a crew
of seat-holders so the sanctuary will never look less than
full. (And even as I write this, I have a nagging suspicion
that's already happened. Have you ever seen a televised
mega-ministry service with empty seats in the audience?
I haven't, but then I can't remember the last time I saw
a televised mega-ministry service, *period*.)

Part of what postmodern Christians — or perhaps better, Christians who are learning to express their faith in
a postmodern world — are saying is that not only do
we need to live what we believe but we also need to
stop pressuring people into doing what God never called
them to do and into being a person God never called
them to be.

Some of the authors in this chapter are part of the
emerging church, but just as many are not. All, however,
fit into a postmodern paradigm in some way or other —
including the secular authors of *Holy Blood, Holy Grail*.

📖 Brian McLaren

A New Kind of Christian

In his popular book *A New Kind of Christian*, Brian McLaren, the undisputed sage of postmodern theology in America, paints as clear a picture of postmodern religious thinking as you're likely to find anywhere. Thanks to this author, I was finally able not only to understand what was going on with my own boomer self but also to find a kindred spirit in the character of Neo, a high school science teacher who helps a struggling pastor regain his faith by questioning it. As I read the book, I kept getting this urge to punch the air with a theological victory fist — one far more satisfying than my old Yankee Stadium versions, since I genuinely shared in this victory. Never mind that I can't articulate my questions and my beliefs anywhere near as well as Neo does; he gives shape and structure and words to those amorphous nigglings at the back of my mind. Come to think of it, "amorphous nigglings" pretty much describes all my thoughts.

Anyway, McLaren's writings certainly speak to all generations of postmoderns, but his gift to boomers is a philosophy based on shared experience. He was there when we were there, trying so hard to believe that we were *it,* the first-century church in modern-day clothing, but all the while knowing that we were missing it not by a mile but by two thousand years. Two thousand years of conditioning that had blinded us to what we could be, how we could have the life we longed for, what it would take to live out Jesus' radical teachings.

McLaren, of course, neither started nor stopped with *A New Kind of Christian.* That's just where I started, and I quickly realized that I needed to back up and read every blessed thing he wrote. Soon enough, he came out with a sequel, *The Story We Find Ourselves In: Further Adventures of a New Kind of Christian,* and once again, I found myself in McLaren's — I mean Neo's — story. Other titles by McLaren: *More Ready Than You Realize; Adventures in Missing the Point: How the Culture-Controlled Church Neutered the Gospel* (with Tony Campolo); *The Church on the Other Side; Finding Faith; Reinventing Your Church;* and *A Is for Abductive* (with Leonard Sweet and Jerry Haselmayer).

A New Kind of Christian: A Tale of Two Friends on a Spiritual Journey, by Brian McLaren (San Francisco: Jossey-Bass, 2001).

John Eldredge and Brent Curtis
The Sacred Romance

It's funny how often I've tried out a new author solely on the strength of a recommendation by a respected friend or colleague. Since many of my friends and all of my colleagues are in the publishing industry, I tend to take their recommendations seriously — mainly because we're all inundated with so many books and manuscripts

that when one rises to the top, we sit up and take notice. One night at a publishing industry event, a trade
magazine editor began talking about John Eldredge, who
was speaking to the group the next morning. *The Sacred Romance* was the best book she had come across in
years, a genuine life-changer. Considering that she had
probably sifted through a thousand or more titles in that
time, I paid attention. Hearing Eldredge speak the next
day sealed the deal: I went out and bought a copy of *The
Sacred Romance*. Then I read it. And then I went out and
bought another copy, and another one, and I don't know
how many more and gave them away to people I love. If
you didn't get one from me, well, there you go.

In true postmodern form, Eldredge sees life as a drama
in which we each play a part. But we've lost heart, along
with our innate sense of wonder and passion, and traded
in our dramatic roles in this "sacred romance" for a life
of duty and obligation — especially *religious* duty and
obligation. In this and his subsequent books, he uses illustrations from popular culture, mainly movies, to make
his point — drama used to illustrate drama. He believes
we all have a sense of "haunting," an aching for and a
distant memory of life as we know it should be.

From Eldredge I acquired a new way of looking at
films, one that has helped me to recognize the under-
lying spirituality in so many secular movies. If more
evangelicals would listen to Eldredge, there would be

fewer outcries against so much of what Hollywood produces. Eldredge introduced me to a wonderful movie, *Enchanted April*, which perfectly illustrates the tension between a duty-obligation life and its counterpart, the wonder-passion life we want and need to live.

Co-author Brent Curtis died in a hiking accident right around the time *The Sacred Romance* was released, and Eldredge somewhat reluctantly resumed their writing ministry alone. If he hadn't — if he had lost heart in the midst of his grief over the loss of his best friend and writing partner — we wouldn't have had the follow-up title, *The Journey of Desire: Searching for the Life We've Only Dreamed Of*, which is every bit as good as *The Sacred Romance*, or the controversial *Wild at Heart*, which, if you believe what you read on the Internet, inspired countless men to chuck their jobs and trek across the country, their women and young'uns in tow, to seek out adventure in the wild, wild west. I don't know. Maybe the rumors of this mass migration are true, and we were just distracted by some steamy Washington scandal at the time.

I love this passage from *The Journey of Desire,* which so beautifully sums up what drives John Eldredge: "Something awful has happened, something terrible. Something worse, even, than the fall of man. For in that greatest of all tragedies, we merely lost Paradise — and with it, everything that made life worth living. What has happened since is unthinkable: we've gotten used to it." Everything Eldredge writes, everything he teaches, everything he preaches, is aimed at getting us un-used to the loss of everything that makes life worth living.

The Sacred Romance: Drawing Closer to the Heart of God, by Brent Curtis and John Eldredge (Nashville: Thomas Nelson, 1997).

📖 Leonard Sweet
A Cup of Coffee at the Soul Café

The year *A Cup of Coffee at the Soul Café* was released, I was the editor of the trade magazine *Christian Retailing* and attended a trade show in Nashville. Editors and reporters received umpteen invitations to publishing events held each night after the trade floor closed. I looked at my invitations for one of those nights and settled on something called Soul Café, to be held at a local nightspot. That night proved to be one of those pivotal events that blindside you as you're going about your everyday life. In this case, I was going about my everyday work life. I had a passing familiarity with the name Len Sweet, but honestly, the venue was the draw for me that night.

Len took the stage and sat on a stool and talked to the audience in such a casual and conversational way that he won me over immediately. No glitz, no glitter, none of the hype I'd been subjected to for the previous two days. And this was Nashville. Hype city!!!

But it was the content of his talk that held my attention, content based on *A Cup of Coffee at the Soul Café*. He talked a lot about the church and what he saw as a changing model for church that centered on community and shared leadership and genuine opportunities for full participation in the life of the church for everyone. Now that may sound a lot like what church is supposed to be anyway, but from my many decades of churchgoing, I knew those were just words without a whole lot of substance behind them.

You could sense that Sweet was talking about something different, some kind of church experience that broke the mold. Whatever he was describing, I knew *this,* this unknown church experience, was something I had longed for since the heady days of the Jesus People Movement. What he was describing has since come to be known as the emerging church movement, but that night I could only come up with one word to attach to his description: hope. I had not been able to use the words "hope" and "church" in the same sentence for years, unless it was in a context like this: "I hope I get sick or something so I have a legitimate excuse not to go to church tomorrow."

I love the church. I always will. I expect to go to my grave loving the church. I just usually hate going to services. They can be so abominably boring, which I consider a sin. How can anyone manage to make our faith boring? But many have tried, and way too many have succeeded. Usually when I say something like that, someone with an impeccable attendance record who has turned church attendance into an act of idol worship will point a bony finger at me, metaphorically of course, and challenge me with the supposedly thought-provoking accusation that *I* am the problem, not church services! Well, gee whiz, I don't deny that. Of course I'm the problem. I expect church to be real and authentic and life-impacting.

What Sweet started with *Soul Café,* he continued with an impressive number of follow-up books. The only ones I've had time to read — and I use that word loosely, meaning in some cases I just skimmed them — are *SoulTsunami, Post-Modern Pilgrims,* and a discussion-based book, *The Church in Emerging Culture,* in which he was one of the participants and served as general editor. On a long road trip I tried listening to another book, *Soul-Salsa,* on audiotape, but it's one of those recordings that uses sound effects and, in this case, a salsa beat for your listening pleasure. Maybe for yours, but not for mine. I returned the tapes to the library, rewound but unenjoyed.

I have no doubt that all of Leonard Sweet's books are worth reading. He's an important figure in the emerging church movement, an evangelical professor who is not afraid to engage in conversation with people of other faiths and with Christians who have found creative ways of living out their faith.

A Cup of Coffee at the Soul Café, by Leonard Sweet (Nashville: Broadman & Holman, 1998).

Gene Edwards 📖

The Secret to the Christian Life

Has it ever occurred to you, as it has to me, that certain evangelists may actually be subversives working for the other side in an effort to make Christians look bad? Sometimes I find myself wishing and hoping and praying that that's the case. Surely it's the only feasible explanation for the ministry of someone who claims to know God, and speak for God, but preaches the most ungodly notions.

One such evangelist, who, I'm afraid, is not a subversive, was really on a roll one night at a church I once attended. The crowd — such as it was — awoke out of their Sunday slumber and were clearly with him, nodding and amening and encouraging him to "Preach it!" Instead, he blew it, but I think I was the only person who noticed. He shouted, and I quote in a quieter tone, "If you're not praying in tongues every day, you're sinning!" No one but me flinched, as far as I could tell. What a crock. (He followed up with his personal take on the 1996 bombing of the Murrah Federal Building in Oklahoma City: God, he said, was powerless to stop it — which neatly got God off the hook but raised a host of difficult theological problems that have nothing to do with Gene Edwards's book, which, if I'm not mistaken, is my point.)

This evangelist and his milder counterparts have a whole lot to answer for, including placing such heavy burdens on the believing masses that it's a wonder any

Christians are walking around with their faith intact. Which is why we need books, and books by Gene Edwards. Because he cuts through all the you-know-what, all the rules and regulations that our modern-day Pharisees have placed on us — a list of duties and obligations that reduce our relationship with God to reading the Bible, going to church, praying, tithing, and perhaps speaking in tongues. To the pharisaical way of thinking, those activities add up to The Christian Life with a capital TCL.

Enter Edwards and his unfortunately titled book. Had it not been for his reputation and a friend's recommendation, I would not have read *The Secret to the Christian Life*. Given the title, I half expected to open the book and find a list of the usual duties and obligations plus a shocker or two, like standing on your head for thirty minutes a day or fasting for forty days and forty nights once a year, year after hungry year.

But Edwards had me at hello. His purpose, he wrote, was "to move you completely away from the proposition that you *can* live the Christian life and to open up to you a whole new way to experience your Lord. Learn this simple, profound fact: You cannot live the Christian life. Learn that, and liberation is near." Well, now, that was more like it. I'm all for liberation. Recognizing our inability to live "the Christian life," he said, is the first step toward freedom. He wrote on page 28, "It is that constant failure that causes us to drag our nearly lifeless bodies up to the Lord Jesus and say, 'I give up, Lord! I cannot live the Christian life!' *That* will mark the most wonderful moment in your Christian life." He spent the rest of this short book showing what a genuine relationship with God looks like.

I wish I could go back and find every person who has looked so discouraged over a situation in their lives and, in shame, said something like, "I know, I should pray more" or "I should be reading my Bible more." For people like that, who have had religious rule after religious rule heaped on them, this one book could change their lives. It really could.

The Secret to the Christian Life: Fellowshiping with the Living Lord, by Gene Edwards (Wheaton, IL: Tyndale House, 1991).

Brennan Manning 📖

Abba's Child

There's a bit of cross-pollination going on between my readers and Brennan Manning's, which naturally benefits me enormously: he's got millions of readers, and I've got...fewer. It's not surprising that his ragamuffins and my misfits would eventually find each other, just as it's not surprising that I found it nearly impossible to settle on one Manning title to single out as pivotal in my life. *Abba's Child* won out because one of its primary themes is our need for vulnerability and authenticity before God and others if we ever hope to achieve any measure of genuine intimacy in our lives. If nothing else, I do try to live a vulnerable and authentic life, but I confess that it's a constant struggle.

Manning's use of the word "impostor" to describe our false self struck a nerve with me, since I often feel like I'm faking it. What if readers — and editors and publishers — find out I have zero talent for writing? What if fellow believers discover I'm not a very good Christian after all? (See the entry on Gene Edwards's *The Secret of the Christian Life* for my current response to that charge.) What if I've been faking it all my life and I don't even know it? It turns out a whole lot of people ask themselves similar questions, because Manning says the chapter titled "The Impostor" has generated the greatest response from his readers. "Impostors are preoccupied with acceptance and approval," he wrote. "Because of their suffocating need to please others, they cannot say no with the same confidence with which they say yes. And so they overextend themselves in people, projects, and causes, motivated not by personal commitment but by fear of not living up to others' expectations" (p. 34).

Manning is a former Catholic priest who married a former nun, which caused no small amount of controversy back in the day. Before all that happened, though, he spent several years ministering to the poor in Spain and six months in a cave in the desert. After his return to the U.S., he battled alcoholism and spent six months in treatment. Manning's honesty and vulnerability about his own failures are a part of what makes him the friend to ragamuffins and misfits that he is. The other part would be his unflinching message of God's grace and love, which is central to all his other teachings.

Also recommended by Manning are *The Ragamuffin Gospel* and *The Wisdom of Tenderness*.

Abba's Child: The Cry of the Heart for Intimate Belonging, by Brennan Manning (Colorado Springs: NavPress, 1994).

Tony Campolo 📖

Speaking My Mind

Tony Campolo is another of my heroes, mainly because he has taken the heat I so richly have deserved. For decades he's had the guts to speak his mind on all those issues that I've struggled with over those same years. I just seldom had the courage to talk about those struggles in any kind of public setting.

What I love about Campolo is that even after all these years of thinking through hot-button issues like abortion and gay marriage, he never comes across as annoyingly dogmatic. What is most striking, if you're really paying attention to what he has to say, is how grace-filled his thinking is — and how incomplete that thinking is. "I expect to wrestle with some of [the topics addressed in the book] as long as I live and am able to think," he wrote.

It's clear that he's uncomfortable with labels like liberal and conservative, and with good reason. He considers himself an evangelical but has been branded a liberal by conservative evangelicals. But Campolo believes a great many evangelicals share his opinions and his concerns, and I think he's on to something there. I'm not exactly part of any evangelical leader's inner circle of confidants, but I do sense that more than a few prominent evangelicals have allowed Tony Campolo to speak their minds, especially when it comes to, say, over-the-top patriotism and the war in Iraq.

The subtitle of *Speaking My Mind* describes Campolo as a "radical evangelical prophet," and though the author is also uncomfortable with that label, it's one that just may fit him. If so — if the prophet part is accurate — evangelicalism is in for some rocky times ahead. But that's not necessarily bad news — not if the evangelical leaders who have been hiding in Campolo's shadow come out and begin to openly discuss their doubts and concerns about things that were once evangelical certainties.

Some of my other Campolo favorites are *Following Jesus without Embarrassing God,* if only for the title; *20 Hot Potatoes Christians Are Afraid to Touch;* and *Is Jesus a Republican or a Democrat? and 14 Other Polarizing Issues.*

Speaking My Mind: The Radical Evangelical Prophet Tackles the Tough Issues Christians Are Afraid to Face, by Tony Campolo (Nashville: W Publishing, 2004).

Donald Miller 📖

Blue Like Jazz

For months after I read *Blue Like Jazz,* I hounded my friends with one six-word sentence: "You've got to read this book." The more I think about the book, the better it gets. That's troublesome for me, because my first impression of it was pretty much off the charts. How does that happen?

Actually, that sounds an awful lot like the kind of musing Donald Miller engages in. Once I became privy to his musings, I became addicted to them. And like a true junkie, I told everyone else in withdrawal where they could score some Miller musings: in *Blue Like Jazz* and a follow-up volume, *Searching for God Knows What.*

In both books, Miller does what a true postmodern does best: He gives voice to his doubts. And he offers criticism in such a charming way that you sometimes have to go back and reread a sentence or more to make sure it was really the criticism you initially took it for. Like this: "In the churches I used to go to I felt like I didn't fit in. I always felt like the adopted kid, as if there was 'room at the table for me' . . . but I wasn't in the family. It doesn't do any good to bash churches, so I am not making blanket statements against the church as a whole. I have only been involved in a few churches, but I had the same tension with each of them; that's the only reason I bring it up" (*Blue Like Jazz,* p. 131).

Anyway, Miller's essays are gems, start to finish. There isn't a dull one in the lot. Whatever you do, don't miss out on one particular essay in *Blue Like Jazz*. It's titled "Confession: Coming Out of the Closet," and it's the single most talked- and written- and blogged-about chapter in any of Miller's books. If that essay doesn't give you hope for the future of the Christian faith in post-Christian America, I can't imagine that anything will.

Blue Like Jazz, by Donald Miller (Nashville: Thomas Nelson, 2004).

 Thomas Moore

Original Self

"The way out of the dehumanizing effects of modern capitalism and industrialism is not to change the system but to read good books." How about that? All this time, when I thought I was just reading good books, I've been working my way out of the dehumanizing effects of modern capitalism and industrialism. If for no other reason than that, and the fact that I no longer have to feel guilty for not changing the system, I would love *Original Self.* The book, that is. Not my own original self.

Loving my own original self came at a much slower pace, because, as Thomas Moore contends, we've been so disconnected from our original self for so long that we hardly recognize the person we started out to be. Moore opens the book with these words: "Far beneath the many thick layers of indoctrination about who we are and who we should be lies an original self, a person who came into this world full of possibility and destined for joyful unveiling and manifestation. It is this person we glimpse in another when we fall in love or when we idealize a leader or romanticize an artist." When discouraged people bare their souls, it's exactly that sentiment — that they have fallen far short of the possibilities they were born with — that they so frequently express. Moore believes, and has you believing, that restoring the original self with all its original potential is possible.

From page 1 (in truth, even earlier — from the preface), there was no question that this man was speaking the language of the misfit, which is my personal language. I never felt that way while reading his 1992 bestseller, *Care of the Soul. Original Self* is a much more meditative, *soulful* book, made all the more enchanting by Joan Hanley's beautiful woodcuts at the beginning of each of the fifty reflections on "an alternative kind of person, one who lives from the burning core of the heart, with the creativity that comes from allowing the soul to blossom in its own colors and shapes." This book is a true keeper, one you can pick up and read at random. In only a few minutes — each meditation is four pages or less — you'll find enough wisdom to stoke the fire in your spirit.

Conservative Christians may be put off by Moore's references to paganism and mythology, but stuff like that doesn't bother me the way it would have at one time. Still, I understand those concerns, which is why I brought it up. Be forewarned; *Original Self* will not be to everyone's liking.

Original Self: Living with Paradox and Originality, by Thomas Moore (New York: HarperCollins, 2000).

📖 Marcus J. Borg
The Heart of Christianity

To hear the evangelical world talk about Marcus Borg, you'd think he was a one-man threat to the future of the faith and everything that born-again Christians hold dear. Hold it — that description doesn't work very well, since Borg thinks liberals ought to start using the term "born-again." My, my, this could get confusing.

But it won't, not if Borg is part of the ongoing conversation between liberals and conservatives — oh, do I hate those terms! — who are trying to find a place of unity in their thinking about what it means to be Christian. Despite all the bad press he gets among evangelicals, I find him to be genuinely interested in working toward reconciliation among Christians, and nowhere more so than in this book.

Unlike so many Christians in mainline denominations, Borg is unwilling to dismiss those who have a more orthodox view of Christianity. Just as Brian McLaren is leading those who identify with the emerging church movement, Borg is in a strong position to bring liturgical and mainline denominational Christians into a better understanding of what it means to be a Christian in the twenty-first century.

Though I disagree with Borg's understanding of some of the elements of the faith that I consider to be essential — for starters, he denies the resurrection — I do consider him an important voice to listen to as many of us wrestle with our interaction with the postmodern world. *The Heart of Christianity* and his other books, including *Meeting Jesus Again for the First Time* and *Reading the Bible Again for the First Time,* offer insight into both the problems many people have with traditional Christianity and the solutions that have helped those people return to the faith by acquiring a new perspective on being a Christian. Regardless of what you think of Borg's ideas, if you want to understand the thinking of the unchurched in America, his books are a good place to start.

The Heart of Christianity: Rediscovering a Life of Faith, by Marcus J. Borg (San Francisco: HarperSanFrancisco, 2003).

📖 Michael Baigent, Richard Leigh, and Henry Lincoln

Holy Blood, Holy Grail

It's *Holy Blood, Holy Grail* that made Dan Brown a multi-millionaire, not *The Da Vinci Code*. Because if this book had never been written, Brown's novel would have been just another tale of murder and intrigue and theft in the art world. The entire plotline that centered around the supposed marriage of Jesus and Mary Magdalene would have been either nonexistent or unconvincingly presented, because Brown's research for that aspect of *The Da Vinci Code* was based largely on the book by Michael Baigent, Richard Leigh, and Henry Lincoln.

All that was decades in the future when I read *Holy Blood, Holy Grail* during my first pregnancy in 1982. Whether it was due to hormones gone awry or the onset of maternal distraction or an inability to concentrate on anything non-natal, I somehow missed the controversy about the validity of the authors' research. The other controversy, the one surrounding the authors' basic premise, I was well aware of, because when the church really freaks out, you pretty much can't miss it. And the church did freak out, with good reason. Here were three writers alleging that Christianity was basically a sham, and that much of what the church had been teaching — and what every Catholic and Protestant church in good standing had preached as the Truth with a capital T — was in fact a lie.

Well now. This presented quite the dilemma for me. First, because I had no idea how faulty the authors' research really was, and so I had no reason to question their findings — which meant my faith took quite the beating. Second, because the protesters had an awful lot to lose — like everything — and that meant their challenge to the credibility of the book was a tad biased. Third, I'd been warned that if I kept poking my nose into all these blasphemous, heretical books, I'd end up a faithless nomad in the service of Satan himself, walking the earth with nothing but a faint memory of the relationship I'd once had with God. Kind of like Eve after she was kicked out of the garden.

So I thought long and hard and gave the book away, a hardback no less. Actually, that's a lie; I'm not that generous. I lent it to my French instructor and didn't press her to return it. I wanted it out of my life, even though I was continually intrigued by it. And then, one day, just like that, I had one of those rare moments of crystalline clarity: I knew, I *knew* that no research, no theory, no archeological finding, no indisputable evidence would ever shake my belief and faith in Christ. *Because my faith and trust was not based on provable fact.* That, my friend, was a milestone moment for me, that instant of realization that my personal experience with God carried more weight than all the facts and documentation and arguments for or against the existence of God combined. I had made the leap from *Evidence That Demands a Verdict* to a judge and jury of one. Me.

Holy Blood, Holy Grail, by Michael Baigent, Richard Leigh, and Henry Lincoln (New York: Dell, 1983).

Also Recommended

Robert E. Webber / *Ancient-Future Faith: Rethinking Evangelicalism for a Postmodern World*

"The road to the future runs through the past," wrote Webber in this first in a series of books that explore the classic roots of postmodern theology and the path evangelicalism needs to take to accommodate a changing church and culture. Also by Webber: *The Younger Evangelicals: Facing the Challenges of the New World* (2002).

(Grand Rapids, MI: Baker, 1999).

Mike Yaconelli, ed. / *Stories of Emergence: Moving from Absolute to Authentic*

This is a terrific collection of essays by the likes of Spencer Burke, Jay Bakker, Tony Jones, Todd Hunter, and other heavy hitters in the emerging church movement. Each essay traces the dynamics of the spiritual journeys of each of the writers; taken together, they reveal a movement in the making.

(Grand Rapids, MI: Zondervan, 2003).

Louis Markos / *Lewis Agonistes: How C. S. Lewis Can Train Us to Wrestle with the Modern and Postmodern World*

Agonistes means "the wrestler," and Louis Markos presents C. S. Lewis as a man who wrestled with theological issues that we are dealing with in the church today, as the world transitions from modernity to postmodernity to whatever comes next. This is a great analysis of Lewis's thinking.

(Nashville: Broadman & Holman, 2003).

Kathy Coffey / *Dancing in the Margins: Meditations for People Who Struggle with Their Churches*

Kathy Coffey's meditations, poems, and scriptural reflections reach out to people in the margins — those who feel excluded from the life of the church because of factors like gender, age, sexual orientation, political persuasion, personality, and religious beliefs. As a self-described spiritual misfit, I fit right in here.

(New York: Crossroad, 1999).

William D. Romanowski / *Eyes Wide Open: Looking for God in Popular Culture*

Starting with the first chapter, "Christians Who Drink Beer," *Eyes Wide Open* won me over. This book offers a way of looking at pop culture through a grid of faith that avoids the strident anti-Hollywood rhetoric so many Christians have become accustomed to hearing.

(Grand Rapids, MI: Brazos Press, 2001).

Ron Hansen / *A Stay Against Confusion: Essays on Faith and Fiction*

If there's one thing postmoderns understand, it's the power of story. Borrowing a phrase from Robert Frost for the title, Ron Hansen looks at the relationship between literature and religion from the perspective of the writer that he is. This is a wonderful collection of personal essays.

(New York: HarperCollins, 2001).

Robert K. Johnston / *Reel Spirituality: Theology and Film in Dialogue*

This is another insightful book on the intersection of film and faith. Like *Eyes Wide Open, Reel Spirituality* helps Christians process, from a spiritual perspective, the messages found in movies.

(Grand Rapids, MI: Baker, 2000).

Eight

PEACE LIKE
A RIVER

Finding Faith in Fiction Once Again

Like half of the country, in 2003 I found myself involved
in many spirited conversations about Dan Brown's novel
The Da Vinci Code. Only one conversation stands out
in my memory today. I was with a group of Episcopalians — remember, they're generally avid readers —
and most were familiar with the controversy on some
level. One man had remained silent throughout the discussion. When he spoke up, it was to say this: "I won't
read anything that's not worthwhile."

If he said anything after that, I missed it. My mind
had wandered off onto a side trail. Along the trail were
signposts bearing questions — too many questions: What
does he mean, he won't read anything that's not worthwhile? How does he define worthwhile? Does he mean
novels aren't worthwhile? Or does he mean only those
novels whose premises he doesn't agree with aren't

worthwhile? Maybe he thinks that ignoring *The Da Vinci Code* will make it go away.

Whether or not a person reads a particular book, like *The Da Vinci Code*, is not the point. Nor is this man's opinion of what constitutes worthwhile. His comment caused me to reflect on my own attitude toward books and the reading choices I make. Granted, many reading choices are made for me. I review books selected from a predetermined list; I judge books for awards based on other people's nominations; and I read books related to the various projects I'm working on. But once in a rare while, I get to read a book for pleasure.

Below are some of those books. After years of reading only nonfiction, I began reading novels, not realizing until much later how postmodern I had become. Storytelling, as it turns out, is at the core of postmodern thinking. And I began to detect the fingerprints of God all over the contemporary novels I was reading, including some from outside Western culture. Those novels reminded me that there was a whole world of poetry and literature out there that I had ignored since college. That's why you'll find an anachronistic title in the mix: I did not read *To Kill a Mockingbird* until sometime in the 1990s.

Leif Enger 📖

Peace Like a River

Beautiful, simply beautiful — that's the most apt description of Leif Enger's masterpiece of contemporary literature. Susan Howatch, as you'll see later, may have lured me back into the world of fiction, but Leif Enger kept me there and offered me a new standard by which to judge novels — all novels, but especially those with a spiritual or religious theme. I routinely use *Peace Like a River* as an example of the ideal Christian novel in my writing workshops.

Enger's use of the language is superb, as he mixes poetic imagery with down-home jargon in this story of a family in search of their fugitive son and brother, Davy, who is on the lam somewhere in the Badlands of North Dakota. The storyteller is Reuben Land, whose birth eleven years earlier was marked by a miracle: when his lungs failed to function properly, his father took matters into his own hands despite the doctor's reminder that the baby had not been breathing for a full twelve minutes. "Reuben Land," his father commanded, "in the name of the living God I am telling you to breathe." And the boy did.

Over the years, Reuben would be the sole witness to any number of miracles that became the stuff of everyday life for the Lands: "Enough people saw enough strange things that Dad became the subject of a kind of misspoken folklore in our town, but most ignored the miracles as they ignored Dad himself." But few were as significant as those that occurred during Davy's run-in with the law and the family's search for him in the Airstream trailer Reuben's father bought specifically for that search. Enger brilliantly lays out the events of their lives and lets the reader decide whether those events were genuinely touched by the miraculous: "No miracle happens without a witness. Someone to declare, Here's what I saw. Here's how it went. Make of it what you will." Reuben continued, "I believe I was preserved through those twelve airless minutes, in order to be a witness, and as a witness, let me say that a miracle is no cute thing but more like the swing of a sword."

Toward the end of the book is a chapter titled "Be Jubilant, My Feet." Never have I read such an eloquent depiction of...what it depicts. That's all I'll say about it, except this: if I hadn't been convinced before, this one chapter convinced me of the power of fiction to accomplish what nonfiction never could. "Be Jubilant, My Feet" transformed all my murky ideas for nonfiction books on exceedingly difficult topics into viable premises for novels. Not that I'll ever actually get around to writing them or anything, humbled as I am by Leif Enger's talents, but at least I let go of the notion that I could handle those topics in any credible way through nonfiction.

I used to believe we'd never see another Mark Twain. I was wrong. We have Leif Enger.

Peace Like a River, by Leif Enger (New York: Atlantic Monthly Press, 2001).

Mary Oliver 📖

What Do We Know

Writing about poetry is not a task I take lightly. It's so daunting that I seriously considered omitting Mary Oliver completely, knowing I could not do justice to her exquisite body of work. But in the end I could not keep her to myself. Her extraordinary gift needs to be shared with others, even if the one doing the sharing is decidedly ordinary.

The best I can do is point you to a sampling of her poems, along with a bit of annotation: "On the Flats," with its images of the "collapsible" sea, of emptiness, of feeling "sad without feeling lost" amid curious, pure, and wild thoughts about death; the panic and longing of the heart in "Blue Iris"; the "blank, white, glittering sublime," the silence, the loneliness in "Early Snow"; and "Snowy Night," in which snowflakes become "stars filling the dark trees," creating a "poem of the night" ("I love this world/but not for its answers," Oliver wrote).

Two of my favorites aren't in *What Do We Know*, but rather appear in Volume 1 of the 1992 compendium *New and Selected Poems:* "The Lamps," with its beautiful and aching image of the seaside at nightfall, and "At Blackwater Pond" (not to be confused with a prose poem of the same title in *What Do We Know*), where the taste of rain-tossed water is like:

> ...stone, leaves, fire. It falls cold
> into my body, waking the bones. I hear them
> deep inside me, whispering
> *oh what is that beautiful thing*
> *that just happened?*

I know I'm not the only person who hears echoes of God in lines like that, because I first encountered Mary Oliver's poetry during the mealtime readings at a retreat center. Still, her poems have always seemed so much more like prayers than poems to me. There's a sense, I'm sure, in which a great many secular poems are in fact prayers; maybe the difference is that her poems seem to express *my* prayers in words and phrases and images that resonate with my spirit but fail to form in my rather pedestrian mind. Nancy M. Malone wrote in *Walking a Literary Labyrinth* (see the bibliography) about a nun who regularly uses the poems of Mary Oliver, Denise Levertov, and others in her private prayer time. Yes, they really are prayers.

What Do We Know, by Mary Oliver (Cambridge, MA: De Capo Press, 2002).

Adrian Plass 📖

Ghosts

I used to have this theory that you couldn't tell if a book had an impact on your life until it had withstood the test of time. I still adhere to that theory but in a modified form: When a book remains with you on a conscious level and refuses to budge, the required time of testing becomes compressed. *Ghosts* is such a book for me.

The premise of *Ghosts* is deceptively simple: seven members of a church youth group meet fifteen years later for a weekend reunion at a haunted house in England, now owned by a woman named Angela, who is both the reunion organizer and a close friend of the recently deceased wife of one of Britain's most celebrated evangelists, who is also one of the weekend guests. Lest you think you know where this is going, let me assure you that you don't. This is no predictable genre novel. From page one, you sense that this is a literary work by an author with an extraordinary understanding of God, human nature, and the erosion and recovery of faith.

It's been several years since I read *Ghosts,* and Adrian Plass's depiction of fresh grief continues to — yes — haunt me. "The one who was half of your existence is gone but... [she leaves] tiny marks or footprints all over your house, your heart, and your life. For a long time these marks of passing are to be found everywhere, every day. . . . These tiny museums of personal randomness are all that is left to me."

So why haven't you heard about this masterpiece of contemporary religious fiction before now? Probably because one or two of Adrian Plass's characters occasionally use words and phrases that just aren't uttered in evangelical novels in America. Ironically, *Ghosts* was published by an evangelical house but only after it achieved widespread success in England, where it was originally published and where it seems evangelical readers have a greater tolerance for "language." *Ghosts* did not do as well on this side of the pond.

Sorrow and abandonment, faith and doubt, profound spiritual truth and psychological insight — Plass expresses it all with a grace and elegance that betray his love of the language. This little-known gem is worth whatever effort it takes to track down a copy.

Ghosts: The Story of a Reunion, by Adrian Plass (Grand Rapids, MI: Zondervan, 2003).

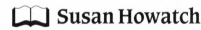 Susan Howatch

Starbridge Series

For more than a decade of my adult life, I lived and read by the credo that life was too short for fiction. Other than a few Robert Ludlum thrillers that inexplicably kept me company through both pregnancies and the classics I read to and with my children as they got older, I read precious few novels. Life was serious, life was important, life was a matter of life and death. Nonfiction — those were the only books worth reading. Nonfiction taught you things, things that could change your life and make you a better person and give you something to talk about at all those parties you were never invited to if you were me. Plus, all the good novels, the *real* literature, had been written before 1950, the year I was born, which for some reason I arbitrarily designated as a milestone literary year.

Then my friend Angie the Jaded Believer began trying to convince me of the merits of fiction. She and I had shared more than a few conversations about the dreadful state of evangelical Christian fiction, the time being the early '90s and all. So when she started talking about a series that had something to do with faith and the Church of England and God and everything, I forced myself to listen. She called it the "Starbridge" series and mentioned that it was written by a British author, Susan Howatch.

Susan Howatch? *Susan Howatch?* The same Susan Howatch who wrote those English sagas back in the '70s, books like *Cashelmara* and *Penmarric?* The books one of my ex-in-laws insisted I read?

Yes, this was the same Susan Howatch, and I'm glad I got over my initial unwillingness to ever read anything else by her. Not because I didn't like those books back in the '70s but because I didn't like the '70s, or rather the part of the '70s I associate with her books. Twenty years later, as it turned out, Susan Howatch's books became a mainstay on my nightstand for several years. Howatch had taken her earlier gift for creating complex, multi-layered stories and used it to present complex theological and psychological truths in six difficult-to-put-down volumes.

There's no telling how much of an impact these books have had on my life, but I know it's been immense. They brought me back into the fiction-reading fold and convinced me that fiction could be used to reveal the deeper truths of life more effectively than nonfiction could. The series also ignited my curiosity about the Church of England, which I would later come into fellowship with through the Episcopal Church. And it was the Starbridge series that introduced me to the concept of spiritual direction, a practice unfamiliar to most evangelicals. That alone was worth whatever it took to overcome those disco-era nightmares and give Howatch another try. Inspired by the series, I found a spiritual director of my own and discovered a rich and rewarding experience.

The series is brilliant, positively brilliant. Start with the first title, *Glittering Images*, and read them in order: *Glamorous Powers, Ultimate Prizes, Scandalous Risks, Mystical Paths,* and *Absolute Truths.*

Glittering Images, by Susan Howatch (New York: Knopf, 1987).

📖 Yann Martel

Life of Pi

It was just too delicious: with some trepidation, I mentioned *Life of Pi* during a workshop at a highly evangelical Christian writers' conference, privately wondering whether I would ever be invited back. After all, this is a book about a Hindu-Muslim Christian (or is he a Christian-Hindu Muslim?) — not your usual fare in an evangelical environment. Little did I know that three rooms away, a colleague teaching another class was also talking about Yann Martel's book. You really need no further evidence that the times, they have a-changed, especially considering we've both been invited back to teach.

Life of Pi is the quintessential postmodern novel, and not just because of Pi's unusual mix of religious faith. The story follows the odyssey of sixteen-year-old Pi, whose family plans to move to Canada from the town in India where his father works as the zookeeper. Alas, their ship sinks, and Pi finds himself adrift on a lifeboat in the middle of the Pacific. His only companions are several of the animals, including Richard Parker, a 450-pound Bengal tiger. Richard Parker aside, Pi survives the 227-day, trans-Pacific crossing (you know that from the start, so this is no spoiler).

If that sounds improbable, all I can say is that Martel is such a creative, intelligent, inventive storyteller that you become a believer despite yourself and the implausibility of the story line. What makes it such a postmodern classic is the make-your-own-reality twist at the end. It's a totally engaging, delightful, sometimes hilarious romp through deep and treacherous waters that had me wanting to believe that the story was true. Well, I mean factual. As with all great fiction, *Life of Pi* is true, in that it is authentic.

Like C. S. Lewis and Anne Lamott, Pi was a reluctant convert to Christianity. His first understanding of Jesus left him feeling that if Jesus was the son of God, he was a son on too human a scale. But the more discussions he had about Jesus with the local priest, the more compelling Christ became: "He bothered me, this son. Every day I burned with greater indignation against Him, found more flaws to Him. I couldn't get Him out of my head. Still can't. I spent three solid days thinking about Him. The more He bothered me, the less I could forget Him. And the more I learned about Him, the less I wanted to leave Him," Pi says. When he finally tells the priest he wants to become a Christian, the priest assures him he already is. "I entered the church, without fear this time, for it was now my own house too. I offered prayers to Christ, who is alive. Then I raced down the hill on the left and raced up the hill on the right — to offer thanks to Lord Krishna for having put Jesus of Nazareth, whose humanity I found so compelling, in my way" (pp. 56–58).

If that doesn't at least make you smile, you're taking your religion way too seriously.

Life of Pi, by Yann Martel (San Diego: Harcourt, 2001).

Umberto Eco 📖

The Name of the Rose

Most avid readers regularly get on a kick of some kind or other, but my reading kicks quickly turn to obsessions. Few things have both fueled and satisfied those obsessions like our county library, whose professional librarians must rue the day they gave me a free ride on the superhighway otherwise known as the database of the library's holdings. Ever since, I've behaved in a most wanton manner, searching the titles, reserving the titles, picking up the titles, and forgetting to return the titles. I could have bought some books three times over with the money I've paid in fines. The librarians made it so all-fired easy for me to access their entire stock that I just went ahead and helped myself. Not long ago, the library system reduced from thirty to twenty the number of books any one patron could have out at one time. I'm not saying the change was entirely my fault, but I do suspect they figured out that my husband and two daughters were not the true borrowers of thirty books each on such esoteric topics as ancient faith traditions, book promotion for authors, and health issues for women in mid-life.

And monastic life. That was one topic that I thought I had pretty well exhausted by 1999. I'd worked my way through most nonfiction books on monasteries, plus a fair number of novels — Peter Tremayne's Sister Fidelma series, for example, and the Brother Caedfael books, which were far better as BBC adaptations than they were in print. Still, they centered around monastic life, so I dutifully read each and every one.

As it turned out, the database wasn't a precise tool when it came to searching for fiction titles, because the search engine missed a host of great books. Among those was *The Name of the Rose*, which I consider the best of the best books on monastic life. The only way I knew about it, though, was through a friend's recommendation. When I read that it was set in the 1300s and incorporated historical fact into a fictional mystery, I was sold; I'd read most of Barbara Tuchman's book on the "calamitous fourteenth century," *A Distant Mirror*, and was already intrigued by that time in European history.

History is important here, because without at least some interest in history — enough to keep you reading through a fair amount of exposition — most readers won't make it past the first fifty or so pages of this five-hundred page novel. Umberto Eco as a writer reminds me of my Shakespeare professor, whose deskside manner was rather tedious all through the first semester but who utterly came to life in the second, rewarding those students who stuck with him with a glimpse into his brilliant mind, extraordinary wit, and flair for the dramatic. I was one of the fortunate ones back then, and I know I'm among the fortunate ones today who managed to stay with Eco.

Eco's complex novel incorporates so many elements that it's difficult to know where to begin in describing it. There's the murder mystery that keeps the story moving along, but that's hardly a simple story line, what with monks dying on a daily basis in a manner that parallels the Seven Seals of the biblical book of Revelation. The primary sleuth is one William of Baskerville (an obvious nod to Sherlock Holmes), a Franciscan who has been summoned to a monastery in Italy for what amounts to a church-state conference. He and Adso of Melk, a novice and his traveling companion, become involved in an investigation into the murders. Sherlock— I mean William — so frequently stops to explain things to his aide that I half expected him at any point to say, "Elementary, my dear Adso!"

Enough about the mystery, except this one critical fact — the murders are linked to a single book in the monastery's labyrinthine library, which is off limits and looms ominously over the entire story. Amid all this intrigue, Eco manages to insert some of the most engaging philosophical and religious debates you're likely to ever find in a novel. The book is rife with literary and religious allusions, including an entire sex scene that draws on phrases taken directly from the Song of Solomon.

Oh, and Eco sprinkles a decent amount of Latin throughout the book, but don't let that deter you. *The Name of the Rose* is worth whatever work it takes to get through it. Did I mention that it also sheds light on the latter half of the twentieth century? *A Distant Mirror* indeed.

The Name of the Rose, by Umberto Eco (San Diego: Harcourt, 1980).

 Hafiz

The Gift

The man who wrote under the name Hafiz was a fourteenth-century Sufi master, which basically means few people knew who he was, the time and place being medieval Persia and all. Henry S. Mindlin, who knows about these things, wrote in the introduction to this volume of Hafiz's poetry that radical Islamics ruled supreme at that time and had a particular distaste for Sufism and its adherents, who claimed that God was directly knowable and that their brand of mysticism transcended Islam. The radicals should have liked the guy, though, since he chose the pen name "Hafiz" — a title given to anyone who had memorized the Koran in its entirety.

I could get all theological here in an effort to justify my reading of Islamic poetry to the religious thought police. My standard response to the thought police these days is much like the one the "man born blind" gave to the Pharisees in John 9:25 when they grilled him about Jesus: "I don't know if he is a sinner. One thing I do know: I was blind and now I see." I don't know what Hafiz's concept of God was in fourteenth-century Persia. One thing I do know: the God I worship is the God I see in many of his poems.

Translator Daniel Ladinsky wrote this in the preface to *The Gift:* "Every line of Hafiz that I have wept over — and there have been many — increased my desire to impart his remarkable qualities: an audacious encouragement, his outrageous onslaught of love, a transforming knowledge and generosity, his sweet-playful exuberant genius that is unparalleled in world literature" (p. 6). I would underscore the playful exuberance part. A single poem by Hafiz can accomplish more than a double dose of Prozac ever could. Not that I would know or anything.

Hafiz is believed to have written as many as seven thousand poems. Less than seven hundred survived the wrath of angry fundamentalists who tried to destroy his life's work. Here's one, titled "This One Is Mine":

> Someone put
> You on a slave block

And the unreal bought
You.

Now I keep coming to your owner
Saying,

"This one is mine."

You often overhear us talking
And this can make your heart leap
With excitement.

Don't worry,
I will not let sadness
Possess you.

I will gladly borrow all the gold
I need

To get you
Back.

The Gift: Poems, by Hafiz, the Great Sufi Master. Translations by Daniel Ladinsky (New York: Penguin, 1999).

 Harper Lee

To Kill a Mockingbird

I once heard author Silas House say his publisher objected to the proposed title for one of his books. The title was *A Parchment of Leaves,* and the publisher said it didn't make sense; people wouldn't buy a book if they didn't understand the title. The author countered with something like this: "Well, who on earth knew what *To Kill a Mockingbird* meant?" His book was published with his preferred title intact.

It's surprising that I made it all the way through high school and college without ever finding Harper Lee's book on a course reading list. Then again, that would have been in the 1960s and '70s, and even those who were on the Negroes' side in this book occasionally said things that were not politically correct in racially tense America. I read the book only after I realized I had no choice but to become a writer, and this was the book that topped many must-read lists for writers. After I read it, I realized that this came as close to the perfect novel as I was ever likely to find. And it only gets better with repeated readings. It's also one of the rarities of print-to-film history — a book that didn't take a hit when filmmakers got hold of it.

For those who missed it in school, *To Kill a Mockingbird* is set in a small town in the South during the Depression. The action centers on a rape trial in which a black man has been unjustly accused of raping a white woman, which naturally pits most of the town against defense attorney Atticus Finch, the wise, level-headed, and compassionate father of the narrator, an eight-year-old girl named Scout (who, I might add, has about the same regard for school as I have, and for the same reasons). Though the town shows its worst side in the conflict surrounding the alleged rape, Lee poignantly shows the gentler side of the Finches' neighborhood. Things get ugly at times, no doubt about it, but ultimately there's that universal message of hope staring you in the face at the end.

Like a lot of readers, I at first bemoaned the fact that Lee never published another book. Surely we've missed out on a wealth of literary treasures she could have produced. But then I realized this: *To Kill a Mockingbird* is more than enough.

To Kill a Mockingbird, by Harper Lee (New York: Warner Books, 1982).

Barbara Kingsolver
The Poisonwood Bible

To a child growing up in the 1950s, especially to a child whose father was addicted to television news, the words "Belgian Congo" were synonymous with raw, ruthless danger. Night after night, as we ate our 1950s supper, perfectly balanced atop the proverbial food pyramid, we listened to accounts of an upheaval that threatened to topple not just the government of the Congo but also the entire continent of Africa. So maybe that's not exactly what the newsmen said, but it sure sounded that ominous to me at the time. Memories of that brutal time in history came back to me full force through Barbara

Kingsolver's *The Poisonwood Bible,* which relates the parallel stories of a missionary family intent on saving a country's heathens and the country striving to save itself from civil war.

There's a lot going on in this book, with the story told from the alternating perspectives of the four missionary daughters and occasionally their mother, over a period of thirty years. During that time, the family has seen more than its share of tragedy and heartache, much of it caused by its overbearing patriarch, Nathan Price, who in technical terms would be called a jerk. He's the worst kind of religious fanatic — a spiritual bully whose way is the *only* way. He wreaks havoc on both his family and the Congolese, with tragic consequences.

Not surprisingly, the spiritual lesson centers on the harmful results of religious shortsightedness. What saves *The Poisonwood Bible* from being a diatribe against traditional religious faith is the introduction of a missionary who uses Congolese symbols, traditions, and culture to teach and minister to the people, in contrast to Price's method of attempting to impose Western culture and a Western understanding of faith on the Congolese. Price's failure is inevitable.

Meanwhile, the escalating tension between the government and the rebels provides a fitting counterpart to the missionaries' activities by showing the detrimental — okay, horrific — effects of colonial rule. The political turmoil caused by outside interference is so vividly portrayed that I remember being tempted to surreptitiously leave copies in the libraries of a few churches whose pastors I thought could use a bit of an education.

This is a beautiful, sad, moving book. Don't be surprised if you recognize Nathan Price as you're reading it.

The Poisonwood Bible, by Barbara Kingsolver (New York: HarperCollins, 1998).

Also Recommended

Wendell Berry / *A Timbered Choir*

Wendell Berry suggests these poems be read in silence and solitude, the environment in which they were written. Each is a meditation composed during the Sabbath walks Berry took over a two-decade period. It's an exceptional poetry collection.

(Washington, DC: Counterpoint, 1998).

Keith Kachtick / *Hungry Ghost*

Hungry Ghost is an amazing novel that's not for anyone who is offended by graphic sex scenes. Those scenes are important, the book being about the redemption of a womanizing Buddhist who meets his match in a Roman Catholic virgin determined to stay that way. You'll probably find yourself very discouraged at one point, but hang in there. Reading to the end is worth it, well worth it.

(New York: HarperCollins, 2003).

Recommended Books
about Books

Basbanes, Nicholas A. *A Gentle Madness: Bibliophiles, Bibliomanes, and the Eternal Passion for Books*. New York: Henry Holt, 1995.

——— . *A Splendor of Letters: The Permanence of Books in an Impermanent World*. New York: HarperCollins, 2003.

Denby, David. *Great Books: My Adventure with Homer, Rousseau, Woolf, and Other Indestructible Writers of the Western World*. New York: Simon and Schuster, 1996.

Dirda, Michael. *Bound to Please: An Extraordinary One-Volume Literary Education*. New York: W. W. Norton & Company, 2005.

Kaplan, Rob, and Harold Rabinowitz, eds. *Speaking of Books: The Best Things Ever Said about Books and Book Collecting*. New York: Crown Publishers, 2001.

Larsen, Scott, ed. *Indelible Ink: 22 Prominent Christian Leaders Discuss the Books that Shape Their Faith*. Colorado Springs: WaterBrook Press, 2003.

The Literary Almanac: The Best of the Printed Word 1900 to the Present. Kansas City: Andrews McMeel Publishing, 1997.

Malone, Nancy M. *Walking a Literary Labyrinth: The Spirituality of Reading*. New York: Riverhead Books, 2003.

May, John R. *Nourishing Faith Through Fiction: Reflections of the Apostles' Creed in Literature and Film*. Franklin, WI: Sheed & Ward, 2001.

Petroski, Henry. *The Book on the Bookshelf*. New York: Alfred A. Knopf, 1999.

Schwartz, Ronald B. *For the Love of Books: 115 Celebrated Writers on the Books they Love Most*. New York: Berkley Books, 2000.

Seymour-Smith, Martin. *The 100 Most Influential Books Ever Written: The History of Thought from Ancient Times to Today*. New York: MJF Books, 1998.

Van Doren, Charles. *The Joy of Reading: 210 Favorite Books, Plays, Poems, Essays, etc. What's in Them, Why Read Them*. New York: Harmony Books, 1985.

Winokur, Jon, ed. *Writers on Writing*. Philadelphia: Running Press, 1990.

Zane, J. Peder, ed. *Remarkable Reads*. New York, W. W. Norton, 2004.

Expanded Contents

1 / A Separate Peace / Fiction and the Spiritual Search

John Knowles/*A Separate Peace*
Gerard Manley Hopkins/"Thou Art Indeed Just, Lord"
Fyodor Dostoyevsky/*Crime and Punishment*
Francis Thompson/"The Hound of Heaven"
The Poetry of Robert Frost
James Agee/*A Death in the Family*
Franz Kafka/*The Trial*
Nathaniel Hawthorne/*The Scarlet Letter*
Flannery O'Connor/*Wise Blood*
Robert Penn Warren/*All the King's Men*
Bob Dylan
Bruce Cockburn

2 / Rebellion, Revolution, and Religion / Black Power, Social Justice, and Questions about God

Malcolm X and Alex Haley/*The Autobiography of Malcolm X*
James Baldwin/*Nobody Knows My Name*
Introduction to Sociology

John Warwick Montgomery/*Christianity for the Tough Minded*

Margaret Clarkson/*Conversations with a Barred Owl*

Josh McDowell/*Evidence That Demands a Verdict*

Robert Short/*The Gospel According to Peanuts*

Aleksandr Solzhenitsyn/*The Gulag Archipelago*

Sheldon Vanauken/*A Severe Mercy*

4 / Dangerous Journey / The Spiritually Subversive Role of Children's Literature

Oliver Hunkin, ed./*Dangerous Journey*

Laura Ingalls Wilder/*The Long Winter*

Paul Brand and Philip Yancey/*Fearfully & Wonderfully Made*

Ruth Nulton Moore/*The Christmas Surprise*

Ben Carson and Cecil Murphey/*Gifted Hands*

Roland H. Bainton/*Here I Stand: A Life of Martin Luther*

Louise Rankin/*Daughter of the Mountains*

Also Recommended

Quang Nhuong Huynh/*The Land I Lost*

John and Helen Dekker/*Torches of Joy: A Stone Age Tribe's Encounter with the Gospel*

Susan Fletcher/*Shadow Spinner*

Barbara Cohen/*Seven Daughters and Seven Sons*

5 / Sola Scriptura / Legalism, Charismania, and Truth

Jamie Buckingham/*The Truth Will Set You Free, but First It Will Make You Miserable*
Johnston M. Cheney/*The Life of Christ in Stereo*
Eugene Peterson/*A Long Obedience in the Same Direction*
Phillip Keller/*A Shepherd Looks at Psalm 23*
Judson Cornwall/*Praying the Scriptures*

6 / The Cloister Walk / Discovering Liturgy and Female Writers

Kathleen Norris/*The Cloister Walk*
Anne Lamott/*Traveling Mercies*
Paula D'Arcy/*Gift of the Red Bird*
Thomas Keating/*Intimacy with God*
Robert Ellsberg/*All Saints*
Henri Nouwen/*Life of the Beloved*
Book of Common Prayer
Richard J. Foster and James Bryan Smith/*Devotional Classics*
Thomas Merton/*The Seven Storey Mountain*

Also Recommended

Richard Rohr/*Everything Belongs: The Gift of Contemplative Prayer*
Rowan Williams/*The Dwelling of the Light: Praying with Icons of Christ*

7 / A New Kind of Christian / The Emerging Church Movement and an Emerging Hope

Also Recommended

8 / Peace Like a River / Finding Faith in Fiction Once Again

Also Recommended

Acknowledgments

Roy M. Carlisle, Senior Editor: Thank you for sharing with me your vision for this book and for your unwavering commitment throughout its many mutations. You have encouraged me in my writing more than you know. If I ever succeed as a novelist, it will be largely because you saw that potential in me.

Shirley Coe: Thank you for the clarity you brought to my words. Copyeditors seldom get credit for their painstaking work, yet their efforts can mean the difference between a good book and a great book. Your insightful suggestions and careful attention to detail made this a better book than the one I originally submitted. I am grateful to you.

Helpful publishers: I can't name them all here, mainly because my memory bank is roughly the size of a gnat's. But I do recall that a number of publishers helped refresh my memories with regard to certain books and their story lines, particularly those older books that are out of print or hard to find. Special thanks to Herald Press for replacing my long-lost copy of the wonderful children's book

The Christmas Surprise and to Crossroad Publishing for, well, everything.

My family: You did it again. You saw me through the writing of another book without inflicting bodily harm or threatening to leave me. How do you do it? Thank you, John, Elizabeth, and Sarah. You are the treasures of my life.

And a last-minute entry — Liana MacKinnon: Many thanks to you for the care you took in proofreading the final copy. Your sharp mind and eagle eyes caught the kinds of mistakes that make me cringe when I find them in other books. I am grateful to you.

About the Author

On her way to becoming an English teacher, Marcia Ford got sidetracked in 1973 by a job as a reporter at the *Asbury Park Press* in New Jersey. She has been a writer ever since. After several decades as a journalist and freelance writer, and as an editor at four magazines, she turned her attention to writing books. A frequent contributor to *Publishers Weekly* and several Web sites, she is also a public speaker, as well as a teacher at churches and writers' conferences around the country. She and her husband, John, live in Central Florida and have two daughters, Elizabeth and Sarah.

God Between the Covers is her fifteenth book.

A Word from the Editor

I was reading a "roundup review" article by Marcia in *Publishers Weekly*, the trade journal for book publishing in the United States. My first thought was that no one person could actually write an article like this legitimately. Or at least without a lot of interns writing synopses and brief reviews. I apologize; it was a cynical moment. So first I wondered how could one person read all of these books, and then second, how could she write this amazing roundup narrative review of dozens of religious books without help? I was clearly having an ego comparison moment. If I couldn't do what she did, then how could she have possibly done it at all? Now I was being cynical and egocentric. It was a low moment in my spiritual journey, I must admit.

So I decided to contact her and ask her to write a book about all of these ideas that were in her feature article. It was my way of asking for forgiveness and my way of admitting that I wanted to learn from this amazing woman who was an author and journalist. Much to my surprise she thought it was a good idea and immediately said she would like to consider doing it. And, of course, she was

incredibly gracious and funny and warm, and even I had
to admit that grace was abounding.

We did go through a bit of a series of glitches over
the original title that she proposed because it was already
taken, and so her agent and I had to work a few things out.
But eventually my editorial colleague John Jones came
up with an even better title, and we were on our way. I
am an editor who is terrible at coming up with titles for
books even after almost three decades in book publishing, so again I was feeling a bit humbled by the whole
process. The ego hits just kept on coming.

Now the real work began. How in the world were
we going to organize the content of this book when I
wanted a memoir of her spiritual journey clothed in a
series of reviews of classic and important books for spiritual growth and written for a postmodern, even young
audience? We stumbled over this problem a few times in
meetings (usually at an annual convention of Christian
booksellers) and during phone calls. But again Marcia
figured it out. Usually as an editor that is what I do, and
I actually do that fairly well. But not this time. So I had to
stop counting up the blows to my professional and spiritual sense of self. It was a losing battle and clearly keeping
track was not helping.

Then Marcia started sending in pieces of the text.
Since this was a book about the postmodern realities in
book publishing and spiritual reading, she was being true
to form. She was sending in random essays as she did

them. I could feel the smile spreading across my face. This was so much fun to read, and it was going to be helpful to many people as a guide. After reading this book or even parts of this book you will be thinking as I did, "Who is this woman?" And then I imagine smiles spreading across many faces of those who love books. We are the ones who aspire to grow and who discover new contours in the landscape of our personal and communal faith by reading. Now it was the thrills of discovery that kept on coming.

For those of us who know that the right book at the right time can change our life and bring us in closer contact with God, this book will be invaluable to own and reread often. For those of us who open a new book with the thrill of adventure coursing through our blood, this book will become a constant companion. So for all of us I want to say thank you to Marcia for sharing her personal journey of faith and for allowing us to be mentored by those who have mentored her through the ages. I can hardly contain my joy at being involved in the editing and publishing of this book. Happy reading, and in this case I really mean that.

Roy M. Carlisle
Senior Editor

Author Index

Of Related Interest

Karen Kuchan, Ph.D.
VISIO DIVINA
A New Prayer Practice
for Encounters with God

A remarkable new development
in Christian prayer!

Join others today who are finding God's healing,
forgiveness, and love through Visio Divina. In *Visio Divina,* meditative and healing prayer is used with a
particular image that God reveals for the discovery
of hidden wounds and desires. Dr. Kuchan weaves
together practical explanations of this new practice,
along with stories of people who have used it to
overcome shame and anger as they discover divine
acceptance and love.

Karen Kuchan, Ph.D., is the founder and president
of the Incarnation Center for Spiritual Growth
and an adjunct professor at Fuller Seminary in
Pasadena, California.

0-8245-2317-2, $16.95 paperback

Of Related Interest

C. McNair Wilson
RAISED IN CAPTIVITY
How to Survive (and Thrive in)
a Religiously Addicted Family

Actor and humorist McNair Wilson is back with his first new book in over two decades. In this hilarious memoir, he pokes fun at everything from Sunday School to strict sexual mores.

Wilson is a former Disney Imagineer who's currently on the road forty weeks a year giving motivational speeches on "Imaginuity," his self-titled creative brainstorming process. Patricia Fripp, past president of the National Speakers Association, has said this of his seminars: "McNair Wilson's talk on Creativity is one of the most dynamic, profound, and enjoyable talks I have ever heard."

0-8245-2118-8, $16.95 paperback

Please support your local bookstore,
or call 1-800-707-0670 for Customer Service.

For a free catalog, write us at

THE CROSSROAD PUBLISHING COMPANY
16 Penn Plaza – 481 Eighth Avenue, Suite 1550
New York, NY 10001

Visit our website at
www.crossroadpublishing.com
All prices subject to change.

crossroad